Berlitz®

Portuguese

phrase book & dictionary

Berlitz Publishing
New York   London   Singapore

Contacting the Editors

Every effort has been made to provide accurate information in this publication, but changes are inevitable. The publisher cannot be responsible for any resulting loss, inconvenience or injury. We would appreciate it if readers would call our attention to any errors or outdated information. We also welcome your suggestions; if you come across a relevant expression not in our phrasebook, please contact us at: comments@berlitzpublishing.com

All Rights Reserved
© Apa Digital (CH) AG and Apa Publications (UK) Ltd.
Berlitz Trademark Reg. U.S. Patent Office and other countries. Marca Registrada. Used under license from Berlitz Investment Corporation.

Fifth Printing: April 2013
Printed in China

Senior Commissioning Editor: Kate Drynan
Editorial Assistant: Sophie Cooper
Translation: updated by Wordbank
Cover Design: Beverley Speight
Interior Design: Beverley Speight
Production Manager: Vicky Glover
Picture Researcher: Beverley Speight
Cover Photo: All photos Lydia Evans/APA except 'currency' photo Lucy Johnston/APA.

Interior Photos: All photos Lydia Evans/APA except James Macdonald/APA 179; iStockphoto 21, 62, 70, 146, 150.

Contents

Survival

Food & Drink

People

Leisure Time

Special Requirements

In an Emergency

Dictionary

Pronunciation

This section is designed to make you familiar with the sounds of Portuguese using our simplified phonetic transcription. You'll find the pronunciation of the Portuguese letters and sounds explained below, together with their 'imitated' equivalents. This system is used throughout the phrase book; simply read the pronunciation as if it were English, noting any special rules below.

Stressed syllables are indicated by underlining in the phonetics. Portuguese has four accent marks; acute (´), grave (`), circumflex (ˆ), and tilde (˜). Accent marks are used to indicate a stressed syllable, or to distinguish between words with the same spelling but with a different pronunciation and meaning: for example, é pronounced 'eh' (meaning is) and e pronounced 'ee' (meaning and). There are some differences in vocabulary and pronunciation between the Portuguese spoken in Portugal and that spoken in Brazil, although people in either country can easily understand the other. This book is specifically geared to travelers in Portugal, with Brazilian equivalents shown in brackets.

Consonants

Letter	Approximate Pronunciation	Symbol	Example	Pronunciation
b	1. as in English	**b**	**bota**	_baw_•tuh
	2. between vowels, as in English but ofter	**b**	**bebida**	beh•_bee_•duh
c	1. before e or i, like s in same	**s**	**centro**	_sehn_•troh
	2. like k in kit	**k**	**como**	_koh_•moh
ç	like s in same	**s**	**cabeça**	kuh•_beh_•suh
ch	like sh in shower	**sh**	**chave**	shahv

Letter	Approximate Pronunciation	Symbol	Example	Pronunciation
ó	like aw in paw	aw	história	ee·_staw_·ree·uh
ô	like u in put	oah	avô	uh·_voah_
u	1. like oo in boo	oo	uva	_oo_·vuh
	2. silent after g and q		guerra	_geh_·rruh
ú	like oo in boo	oo	úmido	_oo_·mee·thoo

When a vowel has an accent, you must stress the syllable in the word that contains the accented vowel.

Nasal Sounds

Some nasal sounds are produced when a vowel is followed by the letter m. This nasal sound is also found when a combination of certain vowels are used (ãe, ão, õe). These nasal sounds produce either an ng sound (e.g., tying) or an oam sound (e.g., foam) with the speaker barely pronouncing the g or m.

Letter	Approximate Pronunciation	Symbol	Example	Pronunciation
ãe	like ayin in saying	eng	mãe	meng
ão	like oam in foam	ohm	cão	kohm
õe	like oing in boing	oing	milhões	mee·_lyoings_
am	at the end of a word, like oam in foam otherwise not nasal: see page 8	ohm	falam	_fah_·loam
om	like ong in gong	ohng	som	sohng

Letter	Approximate Pronunciation	Symbol	Example	Pronunciation
em	like aying in saying	**eng**	**bem**	*beng*
im	like ing in tying	**ing**	**assim**	*uh•sing*

There are over 230 million speakers of Portuguese worldwide. Portuguese is the sixth most spoken language in the world, and there are 188 million speakers of Portuguese in South America alone. It is the official language of Angola, Brazil, Cape Verde, East Timor, Guinea-Bissau, Mozambique, Portugal and São Tomé and Príncipe. Portuguese is also spoken in Macao, though Cantonese is the language of commerce. There are about 400,000 Portuguese speakers in the United States.

How to use this Book

> Sometimes you see two alternatives separated by a slash. Choose the one that's right for your situation.

ESSENTIAL

Where is the market/ **Onde é o mercado/a zona comercial?** *aund eh*
mall [shopping center]? *oo mehr·kah·thoo/uh zau·nuh koo·mehr·see·ahl*
I'm just looking. **Estou só a ver [vendo].** *ee·stawoo saw uh vehr [vehn·doo]*

> Portuguese words shown in brackets are Brazilian.

Pode ajudar-me? *pawd uh·zsoo·dahr·meh*

> Words you may see are shown in YOU MAY SEE boxes.

YOU MAY SEE...

EMPURRAR/PUXAR push/pull
CASA DE BANHO bathroom/restroom [toilet]
[O BANHEIRO]/LAVAROS

> Any of the words or phrases listed can be plugged into the sentence below.

Tickets

When's... **A que horas é...** *uh kee aw·ruhz eh...*
  the (first) bus **a (primeira) camioneta [o (primeiro) ônibus]** *uh (pree·may·ruh) kah·meeoo·neh·tuh [oo (pree·may·roo) aw·nee·boos]*
  the (next) flight **o (próximo) vôo** *oo (praw·see·moo) vau·oo*
  the (last) train **o (último) comboio [trem]** *oo (ool·tee·moo) kaum·baw·eeoo*

Portuguese phrases appear in purple.

Read the simplified pronunciation as if it were English. For more on pronunciation, see page 7.

Personal

Who are you with?	**Com quem está?** *kaun keng ee•stah*
I'm on my own.	**Estou sozinho m /sozinha f.** *ee•stawoo saw•zee•nyoo/saw•zee•nyu*
I'm with my...	**Estou com...** *ee•stawoo kaum...*
husband/wife	**marido/mulher** *muh•ree•thoo/ moo•lyehr*

For Numbers, see page 173.

Related phrases can be found by going to the page number indicated.

When different gender forms apply, the masculine form is followed by *m*; feminine by *f*

Street Markets are an integral part of Portuguese life, but you must get there early to get the full experience. By 10:00 a.m. the best things are gone.

Information boxes contain relevant country, culture and language tips.

Expressions you may hear are shown in You May Hear boxes.

YOU MAY HEAR...

O que deseja? *oo keh deh•zeh•zsuh*
Recomendo... *reh•koo•mehn•doo...*
Bom apetite. *bohng uh•peh•tee•teh*

What would you like?
I recommend...
Enjoy your meal.

Color-coded side bars identify each section of the book.

Survival

Arrival & Departure

ESSENTIAL

I'm on vacation [holiday]/business.	**Estou de férias/em negócios.** *ee•stawoo deh feh•ree•uhz/eng neh•gaw•see•yooz*
I'm going to...	**Vou para...** *vawoo puh•ruh...*
I'm staying at the... Hotel.	**Permaneço no hotel...** *pehr•muh•neh•soo noo aw•tehl...*

YOU MAY HEAR...

O seu bilhete/passaporte. *oo sehoo bee•lyeht /pah•suh•pawrt*	Your ticket/passport, please.
Qual é o propósito de sua visita? *kwahl eh oo prau•paw•zee•too deh soo•uh vee•zee•tuh*	What's the purpose of your visit?
Onde está a ficar [ficando]? *aund ee•stah uh fee•kahr [fee•kuhn•doo]*	Where are you staying?
Quanto tempo vai ficar? *kwuhn•too tehm•poo veye fee•kahr*	How long are you staying?
Com quem está? *kohm keng ee•stah*	Who are you with?

Border Control

I'm just passing through.	**Estou só de passagem.** *ee•stawoo saw deh puh•sah•zheng*
I would like to declare...	**Queria declarar...** *keh•ree•uh deh•kluh•rahr...*
I have nothing to declare.	**Não tenho nada a declarar.** *nohm teh•nyoo nah•duh uh deh•kluh•rahr*

YOU MAY HEAR...

Tem alguma coisa a declarar?
teng ahl·goo·muh koy·zuh uh deh·kluh·rahr

Do you have anything to declare?

Tem de pagar direitos [alfandegários] nisto. *teng deh puh·gahr dee·ray·tooz [uhl·fuhn·deh·gah·ree·ooz] nee·stoo*

You must pay duty on this.

Abra este saco, por favor. *ah·bruh eh·steh sah·koo poor fuh·vaur*

Please open this bag.

YOU MAY SEE...

ALFÂNDEGA	customs
MERCADORIA SEM TAXAS	duty-free goods
ARTIGOS A DECLARAR	goods to declare
NADA A DECLARAR	nothing to declare
CONTROLE DE PASSAPORTES	passport control
POLÍCIA	police

Money

ESSENTIAL

Where's...?	**Onde é...?** *aund eh...*
the ATM	**o multibanco [a caixa automática]** *oo mool·tee·buhn·koo [uh keye·shuh aw·too·mah·tee·kuh]*
the bank	**o banco** *oo buhn·koo*

the currency exchange office	**o câmbio** *oo kuhm·bee·oo*
What time does the bank open/close?	**A que horas é que o banco abre/fecha?** *uh keh aw·ruhz eh keh oo buhn·koo ah·breh/feh·shuh*
I'd like to change dollars/pounds into euros/reais.	**Queria trocar dólares/libras em euros/reais.** *keh·ree·uh troo·kahr daw·luhrz/lee·bruhz eng ehoo·rooz/rree·eyez*
I want to cash some traveler's checks [cheques].	**Quero cobrar [trocar] cheques de viagem.** *keh·roo koo·brahr [troo·kahr] sheh·kehz deh vee·ah·zseng*

At the Bank

Can I exchange foreign currency/get a cash advance here?	**Posso trocar divisas [moedas] estrangeiras/ obter dinheiro a crédito aqui?** *paw·soo troo·kahr dee·vee·zuhz [moo·eh·duhz] ee·struhn·zsay·ruhz au·btehr dee·nyay·roo uh kreh·dee·too uh·kee*
What's the exchange rate?	**A como [quanto] está o câmbio?** *uh koo·moo [kwuhn·too] ee·stah oo kuhm·bee·oo*
How much commission do you charge?	**Quanto cobram de comissão?** *kwuhn·too kaw·brohm deh koo·mee·sohm*
I think there's a mistake.	**Penso que há um erro.** *pehn·soo keh ah oong eh·rroo*
I've lost my traveler's checks [cheques].	**Perdi o meu livro de cheques.** *pehr·dee oo mehoo lee·vroo deh sheh·kehz*
My card was lost.	**O meu cartão foi perdido.** *oo mehoo kuhr·tohm foy pehr·dee·thoo*
My credit card has been stolen.	**Roubaram-me o meu cartão de crédito.** *raw·bah·rohm meh oo mehoo kuhr·tohm deh kreh·dee·too*

My credit card doesn't work. **O meu cartão de crédito não funciona.** *oo mehoo kuhr·tohm deh kreh·dee·too nohm foon·see·au·nuh*

The ATM ate my card. **A ATM ficou com o meu cartão.** *uh ah·teh·ehm fee·kawoo kaum oo mehoo kuhr·tohm.*

For Numbers, see page 173.

YOU MAY SEE...

INSERIR O CARTÃO	insert card here
CANCELAR	cancel
APAGAR	clear
CONFIRMAR	enter
PIN	PIN
LEVANTAR FUNDOS	withdraw funds
DA CONTA CORRENTE	from checking [current] account
DA CONTA DE POUPANÇA	from savings account
RECIBO	receipt

Currency exchange offices (**Câmbio**) can be found in most Portuguese and Brazilian tourist centers; they generally stay open longer than banks, especially during the summer season.

Travel agencies and hotels are other places where you can exchange money, but the rate will not be as good. In heavy tourist areas, you can also find currency exchange machines on the streets. Of course, you should use caution when exchanging money on the street, especially in cities where crime rates are high.

Remember to take your passport with you when you want to change money.

YOU MAY SEE...

In 2002 the currency in most EU countries, including Portugal, changed to the **euro (€€)**, divided into 100 **cêntimos** (cents). The currency in Brazil is the **real (R$)**, plural **reais**, divided into 100 **centavos**.

Portugal	Coins: 1, 2, 5, 10, 20, 50 **cêntimos**; €1,2
	Notes: €5, 10, 20, 50, 100, 200, 500
Brazil	Coins: 1, 5, 10, 25, 50 **centavos**; 1 R$
	Notes: 1, 2, 5, 10, 20, 50, 100 **R$**

Getting Around

ESSENTIAL

How do I get to the city center?	**Como é que vou para o centro da cidade?** _kau·moo eh keh vawoo <u>puh</u>·ruh oo <u>sehn</u>·troo duh see·<u>dahd</u>_
Where's...?	**Onde é...?** _aund eh..._
the airport	**o aeroporto** _oo uh·eh·rau·<u>paur</u>·too_
the train station [the railway station]	**a estação de caminho de ferro [a estação ferroviária]** _uh ee·stuh·<u>sohm</u> deh kuh·<u>mee</u>·nyoo deh <u>feh</u>·rroo [uh ee·stuh·<u>sohm</u> feh·rroo·vee·<u>ah</u>·ree·uh]_
the bus station	**a estação de camionetas [ônibus]** _uh ee·stuh·<u>sohm</u> deh kah·meeoo·<u>neh</u>·tuhz [<u>aw</u>·nee·boos]_
the metro [underground] station	**a estação de metro** _uh ee·stuh·<u>sohm</u> deh <u>meh</u>·troo_
How far is it?	**A que distância fica?** _uh keh dee·<u>stuhn</u>·see·uh <u>fee</u>·kuh_

Where can I buy tickets?	**Onde posso comprar bilhetes?** *aund _paw·soo_ kaum·_prahr_ bee·_lyehtz_*
A one-way/return-trip ticket to...	**Um bilhete de ida/de ida e volta para...** *oong bee·_lyeht_ deh _ee_·thuh/deh _ee_·thuh ee _vaul_·tuh _puh_·ruh...*
How much?	**Quanto custa?** *_kwuhn_·too _koo_·stuh*
Are there any discounts?	**Há descontos?** *ah dehs·_caun_·tooz*
Which...?	**Qual...?** *kwahl...*
gate	**porta** _port_·uh
line	**linha** _lee_·nyuh
platform	**plataforma** plah·tuh·_fawr_·muh
Where can I get a taxi?	**Onde posso apanhar [pegar] um táxi?** *aund _paw_·soo uh·puh·_nyar_ [peh·_gahr_] oong tahk·see*
Please take me to this address.	**Leve-me a esta morada [neste endereço].** *leh·veh·meh uh _eh_·stuh maw·_rah_·duh [nehst ehn·deh·_reh_·soo]*
Where can I rent a car?	**Onde posso alugar um carro?** *aund _paw_·soo uh·loo·_gahr_ oong _kah_·rroo*
Could I have a map?	**Pode dar-me um mapa?** *pawd _dahr_·meh oong _mah_·puh*

Tickets

When's...to...?	**A que horas é...para...?** *uh kee _aw_·ruhz eh... _puh_·ruh...*
the (first) bus	**a (primeira) camioneta [o (primeiro) ônibus]** *uh (pree·_may_·ruh) kah·meeoo·_neh_·tuh [oo (pree·_may_·roo) _aw_·nee·boos]*
the (next) flight	**o (próximo) vôo** *oo (_praw_·see·moo) _vau_·oo*
the (last) train	**o (último) comboio [trem]** *oo (_ool_·tee·moo) kaum·_baw_·eeoo [treng]*

Where can I buy tickets?	**Onde posso comprar bilhetes?**	*aund paw•soo kaum•prahr bee•lyehtz*
One/Two ticket(s), please.	**Um bilhete/Dois bilhetes, se faz favor.**	*oong bee•lyeht/doyz bee•lyehtz seh fahz fuh•vaur*
For today/tomorrow.	**Para hoje/amanhã.**	*puh•ruh auzseh/uh•muh•nyuh*
A(n)...ticket.	**Um bilhete...**	*oong bee•lyeht...*
one-way	**de ida**	*deh ee•thuh*
return-trip	**de ida e volta**	*deh ee•thuh ee vaul•tuh*
first-class	**em primeira classe** business class	*eng pree•may•ruh klah•she*
economy class	**em classe económica**	*eng klah•seh eh•koo•naw•mee•kuh*
How much?	**Quanto custa?**	*kwuhn•too koo•stuh*
Is there a discount for...?	**Há desconto para...?**	*ah dehs•kaum•too puh•ruh...*
children	**crianças**	*kree•uhn•suhz*
students	**estudantes**	*ee•stoo•duhnts*
senior citizens	**os reformados [idosos]**	*ooz reh•faur•mah•dooz [ee•daw•zooz]*
tourists	**turistas**	*too•ree•stuhz*
The express bus/express train, please.	**A camioneta expresso/o comboio expresso, por favor.**	*uh kah•meeoo•neh•tuh/oo kaum•baw•eeoo ees•preh•soo, poor fuh•vaur*

The local bus/train, please.	**A camioneta/o comboio local, por favor.** *uh kah•meeoo•neh•tuh/oo kaum•baw•eeoo loo•kahl, poo fuh•vaur*
I have an e-ticket.	**Eu tenho um bilhete electrónico.** *ehoo teh•nyoo oong bee•lyeht ee•lek•tro•nee•kuh*
Can I buy a ticket on the bus/train?	**Posso comprar o bilhete na camioneta [no ônibus]/no comboio [no trem]?** *paw•soo kaum•prahr oo bee•lyeht nuh kah•mee•oo•neh•tuh [noo aw•nee•boos]/noo kaum•baw•ee•oo [noo treng]*
Do I have to stamp the ticket before boarding?	**Tenho de carimbar o bilhete antes de embarcar?** *teh•nyoo deh kuh•reem•bahr oo bee•lyeht uhnts deh ehm•buhr•kahr*
How long is this ticket valid?	**Até quando é que este bilhete é válido?** *uh•teh kwuhn doo eh keh ehst bee•lyeht eh vah•lee•doo*
Can I return on the same ticket?	**Posso voltar com o mesmo bilhete?** *paw•soo vaul•tuhr kaum oo mehz•moo bee•lyeht*
I'd like to…my reservation.	**Queria…a minha reserva.** *keh•ree•uh…uh mee•nyuh reh•zehr•vuh*
cancel	**cancelar** *kuhn•seh•lahr*
change	**mudar** *moo•dahr*
confirm	**confirmar** *kaum•feer•mahr*

For Days, see page 176.
For Time, see page 175.

Plane

Airport Transfer

| How much is a taxi to the airport? | **Quanto custa um táxi para o aeroporto?** *kwuhn•too koo•stuh oong tahk•see puh•ruh oo uh•eh•rau•paur•too* |
| To…Airport, please. | **Ao aeroporto de…, por favor.** *ahoo uh•eh•rau•paur•too deh…poor fuh•vaur* |

My airline is…	**A minha linha aérea é…** *uh mee•nyuh lee•nyuh ah•ehr•ee•uh eh…*
My flight leaves at…	**O meu vôo parte às…** *oo meeoo vau•oo pahr•teh ahz…*
I'm in a hurry.	**Estou com pressa.** *ee•stawoo kaum preh•suh*
Can you take an alternate route?	**Pode tomar um caminho alternativo?** *pawd too•mahr oong kuh•mee•nyoo ahl•tehr•nah•tee•vuh*
Can you drive faster/ slower?	**Pode guiar [dirigir] mais rápido/devagar?** *pawd gee•ahr [dee•ree•jeer] meyez rah•pee•thoo/deh•vuh•gahr*

For Time, see page 175.

YOU MAY HEAR…

Que linha aérea voam? *keh lee•nyuh ah•eh•ree•uh vau•ohm*	What airline are you flying?
Doméstico ou internacional? *thoo•meh•stee•koo awoo een•tehr•nuh•seeoo•nahl*	Domestic or international?
Que terminal? *keh tehr•mee•nahl*	What terminal?

YOU MAY SEE…

CHEGADAS	arrivals
PARTIDAS	departures
ENTREGA DE BAGAGEM	baggage claim
VÔOS DOMÉSTICOS	domestic flights
VÔOS INTERNACIONAIS	international flights
REGISTO [REGISTRO]	check-in desk
REGISTO [REGISTRO] BILHETE ELECTRÓNICO	e-ticket check-in
PORTÕES DE PARTIDA	departure gates

Checking In

Where is the check-in counter?	**Onde é o check in?** *aund eh oo check in*
My name is...	**Chamo-me... [Meu nome é...]** _shuh_•moo meh... *[mehoo _nau_•mee eh...]*
I'm going to...	**Vou para...** *vauoo puh•ruh...*
I have...	**Tenho...** *teh•nyoo...*
one suitcase	**uma mala** *oo•muh mah•luh*
two suitcases	**duas malas** *thoo•uhz mah•luhs*
one piece of hand luggage	**uma bagagem de mão** *oo•muh buh•gah•geng deh mohm*
How much luggage is allowed?	**Quantas bagagens são permitidas?** *kwuhn•tuhz buh•gah•zsengs sohm pehr•mee•tee•thuhs*
Is that pounds or kilos?	**Isso está em libras ou quilos?** *ee•soo ee•stah eng lee•bruhz awoo kee•laes*
Which terminal/gate does flight...leave from?	**Qual é o terminal para o vôo/a porta do vôo para...?** *kwahl eh oo tehr•mee•nahl puh•ruh oo vau•oo/uh pawr•tuhz thoo vau•oo puh•ruh...*
I'd like a window/ an aisle seat.	**Queria um lugar à janela/na coxia [de corredor].** *keh•ree•uh oong loo•gahr ah zsuh•neh•luh/nuh kau•sheeuh [deh koo•rreh•daur]*
When do we leave/ arrive?	**Quando vamos partir/chegar?** _kwuhn_•doo vuh•mooz puhr•teer/shee•gahr
Is flight...delayed?	**Há atraso no vôo...?** *ah uh•trah•zoo noo vau•oo...*
How late will it be?	**Qual é o atraso?** *kwahl eh oo uh•trah•zoo*

Luggage

Where is/are...?	**Onde é/são...?** *aund eh/sohm...*
the luggage trolleys	**os carrinhos** *ooz kuh•rree•nyos*
the luggage lockers	**os cacifos de bagagem** *ooz kuh•see•fooz deh buh•gah•zseng*

YOU MAY HEAR...

Próximo! _praw•see•moo_ — Next!

O seu bilhete/passaporte, faz favor.
oo sehoo bee•lyet/pah•suh•pawrt fahz fuh•vaur — Your ticket/passport, please.

Tem bagagem para despachar?
teng buh•gah•zseng puh•ruh dehs•puh•shahr — Are you checking any luggage?

Tem excesso de peso na sua bagagem.
teng eh•zeh•soo deh peh•zoo nuh soo•uh buh•gah•zseng — You have excess baggage.

Isso é demasiado volumoso para bagagem de mão. _ee•soo eh deh•muh•zee•ah•thoo vaw•loo•mau•zoo puh•ruh buh•gah•zseng deh mohm_ — That's too large for a carry-on [to carry on board].

Foi o senhor m /a senhora f quem fez as malas? _foy oo see•nyaur/ uh see•nyau•ruh keng fehz uhs mah•luhs_ — Did you pack these bags yourself?

Alguém lhe deu alguma coisa para transportar? _ahl•geng lyeh dehoo ahl•goo•muh coy•zuh puh•ruh truhns•pawr•tahr_ — Did anyone give you anything to carry?

Tire tudo dos bolsos. _tee•reh too•thoo dooz bawl•sooz_ — Empty your pockets.

Tire os seus sapatos. _tee•reh ooz sehooz suh•pah•tooz_ — Take off your shoes.

Estamos a embarcar o vôo... _ee•stuh•mooz uh eng•buhr•kahr oo vau•oo..._ — Now boarding flight...

the baggage claim	**o depósito de bagagem** _oo deh•paw•zee•too deh buh•gah•zseng_
My luggage has been lost.	**Perdi a minha bagagem.** _pehr•dee uh mee•nyuh buh•gah•zseng_

| My luggage has been stolen. | **Roubaram a minha bagagem.** *raw·bah·rohm uh mee·nyuh buh·gah·zseng* |
| My suitcase was damaged. | **A minha mala foi danificada.** *uh mee·nyuh mah·luh foy deh·nee·fee·kah·thuh* |

Finding your Way

Where is/are…?	**Onde é/são…?** *aund eh/sohm*
the currency exchange office	**o câmbio** *oo kuhm·bee·oo*
the car hire	**o aluguer de carros** *oo uh·loo·gehr deh kah·rrooz*
the exit	**a saída** *uh suh·ee·thuh*
the taxis	**os táxis** *ooz tahk·seez*
Is there…into town?	**Há…para o centro?** *ah… puh·ruh oo sehn·troo*
a bus	**um autocarro [ônibus]** *oong ahoo·too·kah·rroo [aw·nee·boos]*
a train	**um comboio [trem]** *oong kaum·boy·oo [treng]*
a metro [underground]	**um metro** *oong meh·troo*

For Asking Directions, see page 36.

Train

Where's the nearest train station?	**Onde está a estação de comboios mais próxima?** *aund ee·stah uh ee·stuh·sohm deh kaum·boy·ooz meyez praw·see·muh*
How far is it?	**A que distância fica?** *uh keh dee·stuhn·see·uh fee·kuh*
Where is/are…?	**Onde está/são…?** *aund ee·stah/sohm…*
the ticket office	**a bilheteira [bilheteria]** *uh bee·lyeht·ay·ree·uh [bee·lyeht·eh·ree·uh]*
the information desk	**as informações** *uhz een·foor·muh·soingz*

the luggage lockers	**os cacifos de bagagem**	
	ooz kuh‑<u>see</u>‑fooz deh buh‑<u>gah</u>‑zseng	
the platforms	**as linhas [plataformas]** *uhz <u>lee</u>‑nyuhz*	
	[plah‑tuh‑<u>fawr</u>‑muhz]	
Could I have a schedule [timetable], please?	**Queria um horário, se faz favor.** *keh‑<u>ree</u>‑uh oong*	
	aw‑<u>rah</u>‑ree‑oo seh fahz fuh‑<u>vaur</u>	
How long is the trip?	**Quanto tempo demora a viagem?**	
	kwuhn‑too <u>tehm</u>‑poo deh‑<u>maw</u>‑ruh uh vee‑<u>ah</u>‑zseng	
Is it a direct train?	**É um comboio directo?** *eh oong kaum‑baw‑eeoo*	
	dee‑reh‑too	
Do I have to change trains?	**Tenho de mudar de comboio [trem]?**	
	<u>teh</u>‑nyoo deh moo‑<u>dahr</u> deh kaum‑<u>boy</u>‑oo [treng]	
Is the train on time?	**O comboio chega a horas?** *oo kaum‑baw‑eeoo*	
	shee‑gah uh aw‑ruhz	

For Tickets, see page 20.

Departures

Which track [platform] for the train to…?	**De que linha [plataforma] parte o comboio [trem] para…?** *deh keh <u>lee</u>‑nyuh*
	[plah‑tuh‑<u>fawr</u>‑muh] pahrt oo kaum‑<u>boy</u>‑oo [treng] <u>puh</u>‑ruh…
Is this the track [platform] to…?	**É daqui que parte o comboio [trem] para…?** *eh*
	duh‑<u>kee</u> keh pahrt oo kaum‑<u>boy</u>‑oo [treng] <u>puh</u>‑ruh…
Where is track [platform]…?	**Onde é a linha [plataforma]…?** *aund eh uh*
	<u>lee</u>‑nyuh [plah‑tuh‑<u>fawr</u>‑muh]…
Where do I change for…?	**Onde é que mudo para…?** *aund eh keh <u>moo</u>‑thoo*
	<u>puh</u>‑ruh…

On Board

Is this seat taken?	**Este lugar está ocupado?** *ehst loo‑<u>gahr</u>*
	ee‑<u>stah</u> aw‑koo‑<u>pah</u>‑thoo

YOU MAY SEE...

PARA AS LINHAS	to the platforms
INFORMAÇÕES	information
RESERVAS	reservations
SALA DE ESPERA	waiting room
CHEGADAS	arrivals
PARTIDAS	departures

The Portuguese railway, **Caminhos de Ferro Portugueses (C.P.)**, handles almost all train services in Portugal and totals 1,771 miles of track. Tickets can be purchased and reservations made in travel agencies and at train stations. You may also purchase your ticket on the train and at various **multibancos** (ATMs). Check out the various special prices and travel cards available (for 7, 14 and 21 days). Rates are cheaper on 'Blue Days' (**dias azuis**), and a 'Gold Card' is available for people over 65.

In Brazil, the rail network is quite small. The Brazilian railway, **Estrada de Ferro Central do Brasil (E.F.C.B.)**, offers few passenger services. The São Paulo–Rio de Janeiro night journey is comfortable but long and expensive.

Can I sit here/ open the window?	**Posso sentar-me aqui/abrir a janela?** *paw·soo sehn·tahr·meh uh·kee/ah·breer uh zsuh·neh·luh*
That's my seat.	**Esse é o meu lugar.** *eh·seh eh oo mehoo loo·gahr*
Here's my reservation.	**Aqui está a minha reserva.** *uh·kee ee·stah uh mee·nyuh reh·zehr·vuh*

Bus

Where's the bus station?	**Onde é a estação de camionetas [ônibus]?** *aund eh uh ee·stuh·sohm deh kah·meeoo·neh·tuhz [aw·nee·boos]*
How far is it?	**A que distância fica?** *uh keh dee·stuhn·see·uh fee·kuh*
How do I get to...?	**Como se vai para...?** *kau·moo seh veye puh·ruh...*
Does the bus [coach] stop at...?	**A camioneta [O ônibus] pára em...?** *uh kah·myoo·neh·tuh [oo aw·nee·boos] pah·ruh eng...*
Could you tell me when to get off?	**Pode-me dizer quando eu devo sair?** *paw·deh meh dee·zehr kwuhn·doo deh·voo suh·eer*

YOU MAY HEAR...

Todos a bordo! *toah·thooz uh baur·thoo* All aboard!

Bilhetes, por favor. *bee·lyehtz poor fuh·vaur* Tickets, please.

Tem de mudar em... *teng deh moo·dahr eng...* You have to change at...

A próxima paragem [parada]... *uh praw·see·muh puh·rah·zseng [puh·rah·duh]...* Next stop...

| Do I have to change buses? | **Tenho de mudar de autocarro [ônibus]?** _teh•nyoo deh moo•dahr deh ahoo•too•kah•rroo [aw•nee•boos]_ |

| Stop here, please! | **Pare aqui, por favor!** _pah•reh uh•kee poor fuh•vaur_ |

For Tickets, see page 20.

Metro

| Where's the nearest metro [underground] station? | **Onde é a estação de metro mais próxima?** _aund eh uh ee•stuh•sohm deh meh•troo meyez praw•see•muh_ |

| Could I have a map of the subway [underground], please? | **Pode dar-me um mapa do metro, por favor.** _pawd dahr•meh oong mah•puh thoo meh•troo poor fuh•vaur_ |

| Which line for...? | **Qual é a linha para...?** _kwahl eh uh lee•nyuh puh•ruh..._ |

| Do I have to transfer [change]? | **Tenho que transferir?** _teh•nyoo keh truhns•feh•reer_ |

| Is this the metro to...? | **Este comboio [trem] vai para...?** _ehst kaum•boy•oo [treng] veye puh•ruh..._ |

| Where are we? | **Onde estamos?** _aund ee•stuh•mooz_ |

For Tickets, see page 20.

In Portugal, intercity bus services are frequent and cover most of the country. Some buses are run by the Portuguese Transport Company, **Rodoviária Nacional (R.N.)**, while others are privately owned.
In Brazil, intercity buses are fairly cheap and comfortable, usually with air conditioning. If you are traveling overnight, look for **leitos**, buses with reclining seats, clean sheets and pillows. Tickets are available from bus stations (**rodoviárias**).

YOU MAY SEE...

PARAGEM DE AUTOCARROS **[PARADA DE ÔNIBUS]**	bus stop
ENTRADA/SAÍDA	enter/exit
MARQUE O SEU BILHETE	stamp your ticket
STOP	request stop

Boat & Ferry

When is the ferry to...?	**Quando é o barco [a balsa] para...?** *kwuhn•doo eh oo bahr•koo [uh bahl•suh] puh•ruh...*
Can I take my car?	**Posso levar o meu carro?** *paw•soo loo•vahr oo mehoo kah•rroo*
What time is the next sailing?	**A que horas parte o próximo barco?** *au qeh aw•ruhz pahr•teh oo praw•see•moo bahr•koo*
Can I book a seat/cabin?	**Posso reservar um lugar/uma cabina?** *paw•soo reh•zehr•vuhr oong loo•gahr/oo•muh kuh•bee•nuh*
How long is the crossing?	**Quanto tempo demora a viagem?** *kwuhn•too tehm•poo deh•maw•ruh uh vee•ah•zseng*

The subway system in Lisbon has four main lines and forty-four stations throughout metropolitan Lisbon. Buy a **senha**, single flat-rate ticket, or a booklet of ten tickets at ticket offices or machines, found in every station.

In Brazil, São Paulo, Rio de Janeiro, Belo Horizonte, Porto Alegre and Recife have modern subway systems, though not covering the whole city. Tickets available are: **unitário** (one-way), **múltiplo 2** (round-trip), **múltiplo 10** (ten trips) and **integração** (one metro + one bus).

Taxi

Where can I get a taxi?	**Onde posso apanhar [pegar] um táxi?** *aund paw•soo uh•puh•nyahr [peh•gahr] oong tahk•see*
Can you send a taxi?	**Pode enviar um táxi?** *pawd ehn•vee•ahr oong tahk•see*
I'd like a taxi now/ for tomorrow at...	**Queria um táxi agora/amanhã às...** *keh•ree•uh oong tahk•see uh•gaw•ruh/uh•muh•nyuh ahz...*
Pick me up at... (place/time)	**Apanhe-me [Me pegue] no/às...** *uh•puh•nyeh•meh [meh peh•geh] noo/ahz...*
I'm going to...	**Vou para...** *vau•oo puh•ruh...*
this address	**esta morada [este endereço]** *eh•stuh maw•rah•duh [ehst ehn•deh•reh•soo]*
the airport	**o aeroporto** *oo uh•eh•rau•paur•too*
the train [railway] station	**à estação dos comboios [trens]** *ah ee•stuh•sohm dooz kaum•boy•ooz [trengs]*

Popular cruises in Portugal run down the Douro and Tagus rivers and all along the Algarve Coast. The Douro River cruise begins and ends in the city of Porto. A cruise of the Tagus River begins and ends in Lisbon. The Tagus cruise will take you through centuries of history emerging from monuments scattered throughout the hills.

In Brazil there are specially organized cruises in all coastal towns for visits to main beaches and nearby islands. Transport between Belém, Manaus and Santarém can also be done by boat across the Amazon River, departing from **hidroviárias** (ferry terminals); for the long night journey, a hammock on deck is preferable to a hot cabin.

Cruises on the Amazon are run by the state-owned **Empresa de Navegação da Amazônia (E.N.A.S.A.)** and a number of private companies.

I'm late.	**Estou atrasado** *m* **/atrasada** *f.* *ee·stawoo uh·truh·zah·thoo/uh·truh·zah·thuh*
Can you drive faster/ slower?	**Pode guiar [dirigir] mais rápido/devagar?** *pawd gee·ahr [dee·ree·jeer] meyez rrah·pee·thoo/ deh·vuh·gahr*
Stop/Wait here.	**Pare/Espere aqui.** *pah·reh/ee·speh·reh uh·kee*
How much?	**Quanto é?** *kwuhn·too eh*
You said it would cost…euros/reais.	**Disse que ia custar…euros/reais.** *thee·seh keh ee·uh koo·stahr…ehoo·rooz/rree·eyez*
A receipt, please.	**Um recibo, se faz favor.** *oong reh·see·boo seh fahz fuh·vaur*
Keep the change.	**Guarde o troco.** *goo·ahr·deh oo trau·koo*

Bicycle & Motorbike

Where can I rent…?	**Onde posso alugar…?** *aund paw·soo uh·loo·gahr…*
a 3-/10-speed bicycle	**uma bicicleta de trêz/dez velocidades [marchas]** *oo·muh bee·see·kleh·tuh deh trehz/dehz veh·law·see·dah·dehz [mahr·shuhz]*
a moped	**uma lambreta** *oo·muh luhm·breh·tuh*
a motorcycle	**uma motocicleta** *oo·muh maw·taw·see·kleh·tuh*
How much per day/ week?	**Quanto custa por dia/semana?** *kwuhn·too koo·stuh poor dee·uh/seh·muh·nuh*
Can I have a helmet/ lock?	**Posso ter uma capacete/corrente?** *paw·soo tehr oo·muh kuh·puh·seh·the/koo·rrehnt*

YOU MAY HEAR...

Para donde? _puh•ruh thaun•deh_   Where to?

Qual é a morada [direção]? _kwahl eh uh_   What's the address?
maw•rah•duh [dee•reh•sohm]

Há uma taxa extra nocturna/de aeroporto.   There's a nighttime/
ah oo•muh tah•shuh ehs•truh naw•toor•nuh/   airport surcharge.
deh uh•eh•rau•paur•too

Car Hire

Where can I rent a car?	**Onde posso alugar um carro?** _aund paw•soo uh•loo•gahr oong kah•rroo_
I'd like to rent...	**Queria alugar...** _keh•ree•uh uh•loo•gahr..._
a cheap/small car	**um carro barato/pequeno** _oong kah•rroo buh•rah•too/peh•keh•noo_
a 2-/4-door car	**um carro de duas/quatro portas** _oong kah•rroo deh thoo•uhz/kwah•troo pawr•tuhz_
a(n) automatic/ manual	**um carro automático/de mudanças** _oong kah•rroo awoo•too•mah•tee•koo/deh moo•thuhn•suhz_

Taxis in Portugal are cream colored or black with a green roof.
Rural taxis, including those at airports, are marked 'A' (**aluguer**)
and are usually without a meter, but follow a standard-fare table.
They are easily hailed in much of Lisbon, and fares are generally cheap.
All Brazilian taxis have meters, except in small towns, where the fare
should be agreed to in advance.
Tipping suggestions: 10% in Portugal and R$ 0.20–0.90 in Brazil.

a car with air conditioning	**um carro com ar condicionado** *oong kah·rroo kaum ahr kawn·dee·seeoo·nah·thoo*
a car seat	**um assento de carro de bebé** *oong uh·sehn·too deh kah·rroo deh beh·beh*
How much...	**Quanto é...?** *kwuhn·too eh...*
per day/week	**por dia/semana** *poor dee·uh/seh·muh·nuh*
per kilometer	**por quilómetro** *poor kee·law·meh·troo*
for unlimited mileage	**com quilometragem [milhagem] ilimitada** *kaum kee·lae·meh·trah·zseng [mee·lyah·zseng] ee·lee·mee·tah·thuh*
with insurance	**com seguro** *kaum seh·goo·roo*
Are there any discounts?	**Há descontos?** *ah dehs·kaum·tooz*

Fuel Station

| Where's the next fuel station? | **Onde é a bomba de gasolina [o posto] mais próxima [próximo]?** *aund eh uh baum·buh deh guh·zoo·lee·nuh [oo paws·too] meyez praw·see·muh [praw·see·moo]* |

YOU MAY HEAR...

Tem uma carta de condução internacional? *teng oo·muh kahr·tuh deh kaum·doo·sohm een·tehr·nuh·see·oo·nahl*
Do you have an international driver's license?

O seu passaporte, por favor. *oo sehoo pah·suh·pawr·teh poor fuh·vaur*
Your passport, please.

Quer seguro? *kehr seh·goo·roo*
Do you want insurance?

É preciso deixar um sinal de... *eh preh·see·zoo day·shahr oong see·nahl deh...*
There is a deposit of...

Assine aqui, se faz favor. *uh·see·neh uh·kee seh fahz fuh·vaur*
Please sign here.

Fill it up, please.	**Encha o depósito [tanque], se faz favor.** *ehn•shuh oo deh•paw•zee•too [tuhn•keh] seh fahz fuh•vaur*
...liters, please.	**...litros, se faz favor.** *...lee•trooz seh fahz fuh•vau*
I'll pay in cash/by credit card.	**Pago com dinheiro/com o cartão de crédito.** *pah•goo kaum dee•nyay•roo/kaum oo kuhr•tohm deh kreh•dee•too*

Asking Directions

Is this the right road to...?	**Esta é a estrada que vai para...?** *eh•stuh eh uh ee•strah•duh keh veye puh•ruh...*
How far is it to...?	**A que distância fica...?** *uh keh dee•stuhn•see•uh fee•kuh...*
Where's...?	**Onde fica...?** *aund fee•kuh...*
...Street	**a rua...** *uh rroo•uh...*
this address	**esta morada [neste endereço]** *eh•stuh maw•rah•duh [nehst ehn•deh•reh•soo]*
the highway [motorway]	**a auto-estrada** *uh ahoo•taw•strah•duh*
Can you show me on the map?	**Pode-me indicar no mapa?** *pawd meh een•dee•kahr noo mah•puh*
I'm lost.	**Estou perdido *m* /perdida *f*.** *ee•stawoo pehr•dee•doo/pehr•dee•duh*

YOU MAY SEE...

NORMAL	regular
SUPER	premium [super]
GASÓLEO [DIESEL]	diesel

Parking

Can I park here?	**Posso estacionar aqui?** _paw•soo ee•stuh•seeoo•nahr uh•kee_
Where is the nearest parking garage/ parking lot [car park]?	**Onde fica a garagem mais próxima/o parque de estacionamento mais próximo?** _aund fee•kuh uh guh•rah•zseng meyez praw•see•muh/ oo pahr•keh deh ee•stuh•seeawn•uh•mehn•too meyez praw•see•moo_
Where's the parking meter?	**Onde está o parquímetro?** _aund ee•stah oo pahr•kee•meh•troo_
How much?	**Quanto é...?** _kwuhn•too eh..._
per hour	**por hora** _poor aw•ruh_
per day	**por dia** _poor dee•uh_
overnight	**só uma noite** _saw oo•muh noyt_

YOU MAY HEAR...

sempre em frente _sehm•preh eng frehn•teh_	straight ahead
à esquerda _ah ee•skehr•duh_	on the left
à direita _ah dee•ray•tuh_	on the right
depois de/ao dobrar da esquina _deh•poyz deh/ahoo doo•brahr duh ees•kee•nuh_	on/around the corner
em frente de _eng frehn•teh deh_	opposite
por trás de _poor trahz deh_	behind
a seguir ao _m_ /**à** _f_ _uh seh•geer ahoo/ah_	next to
depois do _m_ /**da** _f_ _deh•poyz thoo/duh_	after
norte/sul _nawrt/sool_	north/south
leste/oeste _lehs•the/aw•ehs•teh_	east/west
no semáforo _noo seh•mah•fau•roo_	at the traffic light
no cruzamento _noo croo•zuh•mehn•too_	at the intersection

YOU MAY SEE...

Road Signs in Portugal are 'universal,' that is, there is no language associated with them. Here are the most common signs with the English explanation below them:

	proibido ultrapassar	do not pass
	sentido proibido	no entry
	estacionamento proibido	no parking
50	**limite de velocidade**	speed limit
STOP	**paragem obrigatória**	stop
	final de faixa	lane ends
	dar prioridade	yield

A word of caution: outside of major cities, Portugal is mostly mountainous terrain with small, narrow, two-way streets. Overtaking slow moving traffic on the left is permissible, but use caution. At night, when on these unlit winding roads, flash your high beams before every turn to let any oncoming cars on the opposite side know that there's a car around the bend.

Breakdown & Repair

My car broke down/ won't start.	**O meu carro avariou [quebrou]/O motor não pega.** *oo mehoo kah·rroo uh·vuh·ree·awoo [keh·brawoo]/oo moo·taur nohm peh·guh*
Can you fix it (today)?	**Pode consertá-lo (hoje)?** *pawd kaum·sehr·tah·loo (oyzeh)*
When will it be ready?	**Quando estará pronto?** *kwuhn·doo ee·stuh·rah praun·too*
How much is it?	**Quanto custa?** *kwuhn·too koo·stuh*
I have a puncture/flat tyre (tire).	**Tenho um furo/pneu sem ar.** *teh·nyoo oong foo·roo/pnehoo seng ahr*

Accidents

There has been an accident.	**Houve um acidente.** *auoov oong uh·see·dehnt*
Call an ambulance/ the police.	**Chame uma ambulância/a polícia.** *shuh·meh oo·muh uhm·boo·luhn·see·uh/uh poo·lee·see·uh*

In Portugal, metered parking is common in most towns. During business hours there is a 90- or 120-minute parking limit; stick to it or you can get fined. Certain cities have blue zones—streets marked with blue-colored signs where you can pay to park. A ticket machine is usually located in the middle of the block and accepts parking tokens. These parking tokens are available from the police or the Portuguese Motoring Organization (ACP). To park in this zone, purchase a ticket and display it in your windshield.

In Brazil, permits may be sold by traffic wardens or at street stalls. The use of parking lots is advisable in Brazilan cities to avoid parking fines or car theft, and offers to 'look after' your car.

Places to Stay

ESSENTIAL

Can you recommend a hotel?	**Pode recomendar-me um hotel?** _pawd reh·kaw·mehn·dahr·meh oong aw·tehl_
I have a reservation.	**Tenho uma reserva.** _teh·nyoo oo·muh reh·zehr·vuh_
My name is…	**Chamo-me… [Meu nome é…]** _shuh·moo·meh… [mehoo naum·eh eh…]_
Do you have a room…?	**Tem um quarto…?** _teng oong kwahr·too…_
for one/two	**para um/dois** _puh·ruh oong/doyz_
with a bathroom	**com quarto de banho [banheiro]** _kaum kwahr·too deh buh·nyoo buh·nyay·roo_
with air conditioning	**com ar condicionado** _kaum ar kawn·dee·seeoo·nah·thoo_
For…	**Para…** _puh·ruh…_
tonight	**hoje à noite** _auzseh ah noyt_
two nights	**duas noites** _thoo·uhz noytz_
one week	**uma semana** _oo·muh seh·muh·nuh_
How much is it?	**Quanto custa?** _kwuhn·too koo·stuh_
Do you have anything cheaper?	**Há mais barato?** _ah meyez buh·rah·too_
What time is check-out?	**A que horas temos de deixar o quarto?** _uh kee aw·ruhz teh·mooz deh thay·shahr oo kwahr·too_
Can I leave this in the safe?	**Posso deixar isto no cofre?** _paw·soo thay·shahr ee·stoo noo kaw·freh_
Can I leave my bags?	**Posso deixar a minha bagagem?** _paw·soo day·shahr uh mee·nyuh buh·gah·geng_
Can I have the bill/ a receipt?	**Pode dar-me a conta/uma factura [um recibo]?** _pawd dahr·meh uh kaum·tuh/oo·muh fah·too·ruh [oong reh·see·boo]_

| I'll pay in cash/by credit card. | **Pago com dinheiro/com o cartão de crédito.** *pah·goo kaum dee·nyay·roo/kaum oo kuhr·tohm deh kreh·dee·too* |

Somewhere to Stay

Can you recommend...?	**Pode recomendar-me...?** *pawd reh·kaw·mehn·dahr·meh*
a hotel	**um hotel** *oong aw·tehl*
a hostel	**uma pousada** *oo·muh pawoo·zah·thuh*
a campsite	**um parque de campismo** *oong pahr·keh deh kuhm·peez·moo*
a bed and breakfast	**uma residencial** *oo·muh reh·zee·dehn·see·ahl*
What is it near?	**É perto de quê?** *eh pehr·too deh keh*
How do I get there?	**Como se vai para lá?** *kau·moo seh veye puh·ruh lah*

At the Hotel

I have a reservation.	**Tenho uma reserva.** *teh·nyoo oo·muh reh·zehr·vuh*
My name is...	**Chamo-me... [Meu nome é...]** *shuh·moo meh... [mehoo naum·ee eh...]*
Do you have a room...?	**Tem um quarto...?** *teng oong kwahr·too...*
with a bathroom [toilet]/shower	**com quarto de banho [banheiro]/chuveiro** *kaum kwahr·too deh buh·nyoo [buh·nyay·roo]/ shoo·vay·roo*
with air conditioning	**com ar condicionado** *kaum ar kawn·dee·seeoo·nah·thoo*
that's smoking/ non-smoking	**para fumadores [fumantes]/não-fumadores [não-fumantes]** *puh·ruh foo·muh·daurz [foo·muhnts]/nohm foo·muh·daurz [nohm foo·muhnts]*
For...	**Para...** *puh·ruh...*
tonight	**hoje à noite** *auzseh ah noyt*

two nights	**duas noites** _thoo_·uhz noytz
one week	**uma semana** _oo_·muh seh·_muh_·nuh
Does the hotel have…?	**O hotel tem…?** oo aw·_tehl_ teng…
a computer	**um computador** oong kaum·poo·tuh·_daur_
an elevator [lift]	**um elevador** oong eh·leh·_vuh_·daur
(wireless) internet service	**serviço de internet** sehr·_vee_·soo deh een·tehr·_neht_
room service	**serviço de quartos** sehr·_vee_·soo deh _kwahr_·tooz
a pool	**piscina** pee·_see_·nuh
a gym	**um ginásio** oong zsee·_nah_·zee·oo
I need…	**Preciso de…** preh·_see_·zoo deh…
an extra bed	**outra cama** _auoo_·truh _kuh_·muh
a cot	**cama de lona** _kuh_·muh deh _law_·nuh
a crib	**uma cama de bebé [neném]** _oo_·muh _kuh_·muh de beh·_beh_ [neh·_neh_]

For Numbers, see page 173.

Price

How much per night/week?	**Quanto é por noite/semana?** _kwuhn_·too eh poor noyt/seh·_muh_·nuh
Are there any discounts?	**Há algum desconto?** ah ahl·goong dehs·_kaum_·too

All types of accommodation can be found through the **Posto de Turismo** (Tourist Information Center).

In Portugal **Turismo no Espaço Rural** offers privately owned homes ranging from manor houses (**Turismo de Habitação**) to country houses in rural settings (**Turismo Rural**) and farmhouses (**Agro-tourism**). In the Algarve and other seaside resorts, you should have little trouble finding locals wanting to rent a room in their own house.

In Brazil, the cheapest form of accommodations is the **dormitório**, providing a shared room for a few reais per night. Other kinds of lodging are:

Hotel

Hotels in Portugal are graded from 2-star to 5-star deluxe; in Brazil, where most hotels are regulated by **Embratur** (the Brazilian Tourism Authority) there are five official categories.

Hotel-Apartamento

Apartment hotels ranging from 2- to 4-star.

Hotel fazenda

Farmhouse lodges, generally equipped with a swimming pool, tennis court and horseback-riding facilities.

Pousada

A state-owned inn converted from an old castle, monastery, convent, palace or in a location of interest to tourists.

Pensão

Corresponds to a boarding house. Usually divided into four categories.

Pousada de juventude

Youth hostel; there are nearly 20 in Portugal and over 90 in Brazil. In Brazil, hostels are open to anyone, though members obtain discounts.

Residencial

Bed and breakfast accommodations.

| Does the price include breakfast/sales tax? | **O preço inclui o pequeno-almoço [café da manhã]/taxas?** *oo preh·soo een·kloo·ee oo peh·keh·noo ahl·mau·soo [kuh·feh duh muh·nyuh]/ tah·shuhz* |
| Are there any discounts? | **Há algum desconto?** *ah ahl·goong dehs·kaum·too* |

YOU MAY HEAR...

O seu passaporte/cartão de crédito, por favor. *oo sehoo pah·suh·pawrt/kuhr·tohm deh kreh·dee·too poor fuh·vaur*	Your passport/credit card, please.
Preencha esta ficha, por favor. *pree·ehn·shuh eh·stuh fee·shuh poor fuh·vaur*	Please fill out this form.
Assine aqui. *uh·see·neh uh·kee*	Sign here.

Preferences

Can I see the room?	**Posso ver o quarto?** *paw·soo vehr oo kwahr·too*
I'd like a...room.	**Queria um... quarto.** *keh·ree·uh oong... kwahr·too*
better	**melhor** *meh·lyohr*
bigger	**maior** *muh·eeohr*
cheaper	**mais barato** *meyez buh·rah·too*
quieter	**mais silencioso** *meyez see·lehn·see·aw·zoo*
I'll take it.	**Fico com esse.** *fee·koo kaum eh·seh.*
No, I won't take it.	**Não, não fico com esse.** *nohm, nohm fee·koo kaum eh·seh*

Questions

| Where's...? | **Onde é...?** *aund eh...* |
| the bar | **o bar** *oo bar* |

the bathroom [toilet]	**a casa de banho [o banheiro]** *uh kah·zuh deh buh·nyoo [oo buh·nyay·roo]*	
the elevator [lift]	**o elevador** *oo eh·leh·vuh·daur*	
Can I have…?	**Pode arranjar-me [arrumar-me]…?** *pawd uh·rrehn·zsahr·meh [ah·rroo·mahr·me]…*	
a blanket	**um cobertor** *oong koo·behr·taur*	
an iron	**um ferro de engomar** *oong feh·rroo deh ehn·goo·mahr*	
a pillow	**uma almofada [um travesseiro]** *oo·muh ahl·moo·fah·duh [oong truh·veh·say·roo]*	45
soap	**um sabonete** *oong suh·boo·neht*	
toilet paper	**papel higiénico** *puh·pehl ee·zseh·nee·koo*	
a towel	**uma toalha** *oo·muh too·ah·lyuh*	
Do you have an adapter for this?	**Tem um adaptador para isto?** *teng oong uh·duhp·tuh·daur puh·ruh ee·stoo*	
How do I turn on the lights?	**Como é que se acende as luzes?** *kau·moo eh keh seh uh·sehn·deh uhz loo·zehz*	
Could you wake me at…?	**Podia acordar-me às…?** *poo·dee·uh uh·koor·dahr·meh ahz…*	
Can I leave this in the safe?	**Posso deixar isto no cofre?** *paw·soo thay·shahr ee·stoo noo kaw·freh*	
I'd like to get my things from the safe.	**Queria tirar as minhas coisas do cofre.** *keh·ree·uh tee·rahr uhz mee·nyuhz koy·zuhz thoo kaw·freh*	
Is/Are there any mail/ messages for me?	**Há correio [correspondência]/alguma mensagem para mim?** *ah koo·rray·oo [kaw·rrehs·paun·dehn·see·uh]/ahl·goo·muh mehn·sah·zseng puh·ruh meeng*	
Do you have a laundry service?	**Tem serviço de lavandaria?** *teng sehr·vee·soo deh luh·vuhn·deh·ree·uh*	

Problems

There's a problem.	**Há um problema.** *ah oong proo·bleh·muh*
I've lost my key/ key card.	**Perdi a minha chave/carta de chave.** *pehr·dee uh mee·nyuh shahv/kahr·tuh deh shahv*
I've locked myself out of my room.	**Fechei-me fora do quarto.** *fee·shay·meh faw·ruh thoo kwahr·too*
There's no hot water/ toilet paper.	**Não há água quente/papel higiénico.** *nohm ah ah·gwuh kehnt/puh·pehl ee·zseh·nee·koo*
The room is dirty.	**O quarto está sujo.** *oo kwahr·too ee·stah soo·zsoo*
There are bugs in our room.	**Há insectos no quarto.** *ah een·sehk·tooz noo kwahr·too*
. . .doesn't work.	**. . .tem um defeito.** *. . . teng oong deh·fay·too*
Can you fix. . .?	**Pode arranjar. . .?** *pawd uh·rrehn·zsahr. . .*
the air conditioning	**o ar condicionado** *oo ar kawn·dee·seeoo·nah·thoo*
the fan	**a ventoinha [o ventilador]** *uh vehn·too·ee·nyuh [oo vehn·tee·luh·daur]*
the heat [heating]	**o aquecimento** *oo uh·keh·see·mehn·too*
the lights	**as luzes** *uhz loo·zehz*
the TV	**a TV** *uh teh·veh*
the toilet	**a retrete** *uh reh·treht*
I'd like to move to another room.	**Queria mudar de quarto.** *keh·ree·uh moo·dahr deh kwahr·too*

Restrooms in Portugal are labeled W.C. Major cities have public toilets that are automatically sanitized after each use. They are found on the street and have a small fee per use. Some of these public restrooms have 20-minute time limits, and the door will automatically open when your time is up.

In hotels and private residences, it is standard for bathrooms to be equipped with bidets.

YOU MAY SEE...

EMPURRAR/PUXAR	push/pull
CASA DE BANHO [O BANHEIRO]/LAVABOS	bathroom/restroom [toilet]
CHUVEIRO	shower
ELEVADOR	elevator [lift]
ESCADAS	stairs
LAVANDARIA	laundry
NÃO PERTURBAR	do not disturb
PORTA DE INCÊNDIO	fire door
SAÍDA (DE EMERGÊNCIA)	(emergency) exit
CHAMADA PARA DESPERTAR	wake-up call

Checking Out

When's check-out?	**A que horas temos de deixar o quarto?** *uh kee aw•ruhz teh•mooz deh thay•shahr oo kwahr•too*
Could I leave my bags here until…?	**Posso deixar a minha bagagem aqui até…?** *paw•soo day•shahr uh mee•nyuh buh•gah•zseng uh•kee uh•teh…*
Can I have an itemized bill/a receipt?	**Pode dar-me uma conta detalhada/uma factura [um recibo]?** *pawd dahr•meh oo•muh kaum•tuh deh•tuh•lyah•duh/oo•muh fah•too•ruh [oong reh•see•boo]*
I think there's a mistake.	**Creio que se enganou.** *kray•oo keh seh ehn•guh•nau*
I'll pay in cash/by credit card.	**Pago com dinheiro/com o cartão de crédito.** *pah•goo kaum dee•nyay•roo/kaum oo kuhr•tohm deh kreh•dee•too*

The 220-volt, 50-cycle AC is the norm throughout Portugal. If you bring your own electrical appliances, buy an adapter plug (round pins, not square) before leaving home. The electrical current in Brazil is not completely standardized. Some parts of Brazil are 220 V while others are 110 V. Most of Brazil, including Rio de Janeiro and São Paulo, is 110 or 120 V, 60 Hz AC.

Renting

I reserved an apartment/a room.	**Reservei um apartamento/quarto.** *reh·zehr·vay oong uh·puhr·tuh·mehn·too/ kwahr·too*
My name is…	**Chamo-me… [Meu nome é…]** *shuh·moo meh… [mehoo naum·ee eh…]*
Can I have the key/key card?	**Posso ter a chave/carta de chave?** *paw·soo tehr uh shahv/kahr·tuh deh shahv*
Are there…?	**Há…?** *ah…*
dishes	**a louça** *uh lau·suh*
pillows	**almofadas** *ahl·moo·fah·duhz*
sheets	**lençóis** *lehn·soyz*
towels	**toalhas** *too·ah·lyuhz*
utensils [cutlery]	**os talheres** *ooz tuh·lyeh·rehz*
When do I put out the bins/recycling?	**Quando ponho o lixo/o lixo para reciclar lá fora?** *kwuhn·doo paw·nyoo oo lee·shoo/ lee·shoo puh·ruh ree·see·klahr lah faw·ruh*
…is broken.	**…está partido m/partida f[quebrado m/ quebrada f].** *…ee·stah puhr·tee·thoo/ puhr·tee·thuh [keh·brah·doo/ keh·brah·duh]*
How does…work?	**Como funciona…?** *kau·moo faun·see·aw·nuh…*
the air conditioner	**o ar condicionado** *oo ar kawn·dee·seeoo·nah·thoo*

A service charge is generally added to your hotel and restaurant bills. However, if the service has been particularly good, you may want to leave an extra tip. The following chart is a guide:

	Portugal	Brazil
Bellman, per bag	€0.50	R$ 0.35–0.50
Hotel maid, per week	€3	R$ 5
Restroom attendant	€0.20	R$ 0.50–1

the dishwasher	**a máquina de lavar pratos** uh <u>mah</u>•kee•nuh deh luh•<u>vahr prah</u>•tooz
the freezer	**a arca frigorífica [o congelador]** uh <u>ahr</u>•kuh free•goo•<u>ree</u>•fee•kuh [oo kaum•zseh•luh•<u>daur</u>]
the heater	**o aquecedor** oo uh•<u>keh</u>•seh•daur
the microwave	**o microondas** oo mee•krau•<u>aun</u>•duhz
the refrigerator	**o frigorífico [a geladeira]** oo free•goo•<u>ree</u>•fee•koo [uh zseh•luh•<u>thay</u>•ruh]
the stove	**o fogão** oo foo•<u>gohm</u>
the washing machine	**a máquina de lavar (roupa)** uh <u>mah</u>•kee•nuh deh luh•<u>vahr</u> (<u>rauoo</u>•puh)

Domestic Items

I need...	**Preciso de...** preh•<u>see</u>•zoo deh...
an adapter	**um adaptador** oong uh•duhp•tuh•<u>daur</u>
aluminum [kitchen] foil	**papel de alumínio** puh•<u>pehl</u> deh uh•loo•<u>mee</u>•nee•oo
a bottle opener	**um abre-garrafas [abridor de garrafas]** oong ah•breh•guh•<u>rrah</u>•fuhz [uh•bree•<u>daur</u> deh guh•<u>rrah</u>•fuhz]
a broom	**uma vassoura** <u>oo</u>•muh vuh•<u>sau</u>•ruh

a can opener	**um abre-latas [abridor de latas]** *oong ah-breh-lah-tuhz [ah-bree-daur deh lah-tuhz]*
cleaning supplies	**produtos de limpeza** *prau-thoo-tooz deh leem-peh-zuh*
a corkscrew	**um saca-rolhas** *oong sah-kuh-rau-lyuz*
I need...	**Preciso de...** *preh-see-zoo deh...*
detergent	**detergente em pó para a roupa** *deh-tehr-zsehnt eng paw puh-ruh uh rauoo-puh*
dishwashing liquid	**detergente para a louça** *deh-tehr-zsehnt puh-ruh uh lau-suh*
bin bags	**sacos para o lixo** *sah-kooz puh-ruh oo lee-shoo*
a light bulb	**uma lâmpada eléctrica** *oo-muh luhm-puh-duh ee-leh-tree-kuh*
matches	**fósforos** *fawz-fuh-rooz*
a mop	**o esfregão** *oo ees-fruh-gohm*
paper napkins	**guardanapos de papel** *gwahr-duh-nah-pooz deh puh-pehl*
paper towels	**papel da cozinha** *puh-pehl duh koo-zee-nyuh*
plastic wrap [cling film]	**papel aderente** *puh-pehl uh-deh-rehnt*
a plunger	**um desentupidor** *oong deh-zehn-too-pee-daur*
scissors	**uma tesoura** *oo-muh teh-zau-ruh*
a vacuum cleaner	**um aspirador** *oong uh-spee-ruh-daur*

For In the Kitchen, see page 81.

At the Hostel

Do you have any places left for tonight?	**Ainda há vagas para hoje à noite?** *uh-een-duh ah vah-guhz puh-ruh auzseh ah noyt*
Can I have...?	**Pode dar-me...?** *pawd dahr-meh...*
a single/double room	**um quarto individual/duplo** *oong kwahr-too een-dee-vee-doo-ahl/doo-ploo*

a blanket	**um cobertor** *oong koo·behr·taur*
a pillow	**uma almofada [um travesseiro]** *oo·muh ahl·moo·fah·duh [oong truh·veh·say·roo]*
sheets	**lençóis** *lehn·soyz*
a towel	**uma toalha** *oo·muh too·ah·lyuh*
Do you have lockers?	**Tem cacifos?** *teng kuh·see·fooz*
What time are the doors locked?	**A que horas fecham as portas?** *uh keh aw·ruhz feh·shohm uhz pawr·tuhz*
Do I need a membership card?	**Preciso de cartão de sócio?** *preh·see·zoo deh kuhr·tohm deh saw·see·oo*
Here's my international student card.	**Aqui está o meu cartão internacional de estudante.** *uh·kee ee·stah oo mehoo kuhr·tohm een·tehr·nuh·seeoo·nahl de ee·stoo·duhnt*

There are nearly twenty youth hostels in Portugal and over ninety in Brazil. In Portugal, prices for a room at a hostel range anywhere from seventeen to sixty-five euros. In order to stay in a hostel in Portugal, you must be under the age of twenty-six and have a Youth Card. If you do not have a Youth Card, you can purchase one at the hostel upon arrival. The Youth Card is valid until your twenty-sixth birthday. In Brazil, hostels are open to anyone, though members who have a Youth Card receive discounts.

Going Camping

Can I camp here?	**Posso acampar aqui?** *paw·soo uh·kuhm·pahr uh·kee*
Where's the campsite?	**Onde é o parque de campismo [camping]?** *aund eh oo pahr·keh deh kuhm·peez·moo [kuhm·peeng]*
What is the charge per day/week?	**Qual é a tarifa por dia/semana?** *kwahl eh uh tuh·ree·fuh poor dee·uh/seh·muh·nuh*

Are there...?	**Há...?** *ah...*
cooking facilities	**uma área para se cozinhar** *oo·muh ah·ree·uh puh·ruh seh koo·zee·nyahr*
electrical outlets	**electricidade** *ee·leh·tree·see·dahd*
laundry facilities	**uma lavandaria** *oo·muh luh·vuhn·deh·ree·uh*
Are there...?	**Há...?** *ah...*
showers	**o chuveiro** *oo shoo·vay·roo*
tents for rent [hire]	**tendas para aluguer** *tehn·duhz puh·ruh uh·loo·gehr*
Where can I empty the chemical toilet?	**Onde posso esvaziar o banheiro químico?** *aund paw·soo ees·vee·ahr oo buh·nyay·roo kee·mee·koo*

YOU MAY SEE...

ÁGUA POTÁVEL	drinking water
É PROIBIDO ACAMPAR	no camping
É PROIBIDO ACENDER FOGOS/CHURRASCAR	no fires/barbecues

Communications

ESSENTIAL

Where's an internet café?	**Onde fica um internet café?** *aund fee·kuh oong een·tehr·neht kuh·feh*
Can I access the Internet here?	**Tenho acesso à internet aqui?** *teh·nyoo uh·seh·soo ah een·tehr·neht uh·kee*
Can I check e-mail here?	**Posso ler o meu e-mail aqui?** *paw·soo lehr oo mehoo ee·mehl uh·khee*
How much per (half) hour?	**Quanto é por (meia) hora?** *kwuhn·too eh poor (may·uh) aw·ruh*

How do I connect/ log on?	**Como conecto/faço o logon?** *kau•moo koo•nehk•too/fah•soo oo law•gawn*
A phone card, please.	**Um credifone [cartão telefónico], se faz favor.** *oong kreh•dee•faun [kuhr•tohm tehl•eh•fawn•ee•koo] seh fahz fuh•vaur*
Can I have your phone number?	**Pode dar-me o seu número de telefone?** *pawd dahr•meh oo sehoo noo•meh•roo deh tehl•fawn*
Here's my number/ e-mail address.	**Este é o meu número/e-mail.** *ehst eh oo mehoo noo•meh•roo/ee•mehl*
Call me.	**Telefone-me.** *tehl•fawn•eh•meh*
E-mail me.	**Envie-me um e-mail.** *ehn•vee•eh meh oong ee•mehl*
Hello. This is...	**Estou [Alô]. Fala...** *ee•stawoo [aw•lah]. fah•luh...*
I'd like to speak to...	**Queria falar com...** *keh•ree•uh fuh•lahr kaum...*
Could you repeat that, please?	**Importa-se de repetir, por favor?** *eem•pawr•tuh•seh deh reh•peh•teer poor fuh•vaur*
I'll call back later.	**Chamo mais tarde.** *shuh•moo meyez tahr•deh*
Bye.	**Adeus.** *uh•deeoosh*
Where's the post office?	**Onde são os correios?** *aund sohm ooz koo•rray•ooz*
I'd like to send this to...	**Gostaria de mandar isto para...** *goo•stuh•ree•uh deh muhn•dahr ee•stoo puh•ruh...*

Online

Where's an internet cafe?	**Onde fica um internet café?** *aund fee•kuh oong een•tehr•neht kuh•feh*
Does it have wireless internet?	**Tem internet wireless?** *teng een•tehr•neht wire•less*
What is the WiFi password?	**Qual é a senha do WiFi?** *kwahl eh uh seh•nyuh doo WiFi*
Is the WiFi free?	**O WiFi é grátis?** *oo WiFi eh grah teez*
Do you have bluetooth?	**Tem bluetooth?** *teng bluetooth*

How do I turn the computer on/off?	**Como ligo/desligo o computador?** _kau·moo lee·goo/dehz·lee·goo oo kaum·poo·tuh·daur_
Can I...?	**Posso...?** _paw·soo..._
access the internet	**aceder a internet** _uh·seh·dehr uh een·tehr·neht_
check e-mail	**ler o meu e-mail** _lehr oo mehoo ee·mehl_
print	**imprimir [impressar]** _eeng·pree·meer [eeng·preh·sahr]_
How much per (half) hour?	**Quanto é por (meia) hora?** _kwuhn·too eh poor (may·uh) aw·ruh_
How do I...?	**Como...?** _kau·moo..._
connect/disconnect	**conecto/desconecto** _koo·nehk·too/dehz·koo·nehk·too_
log on/off	**faço o logon/logoff** _fah·soo oo law·gawn/law·gawf_
type this symbol	**bato este símbolo** _bah·too ehst seem·boo·loo_
What's your e-mail?	**Qual é o seu e-mail?** _kwahl eh oo sehoo ee·mehl_
My e-mail is...	**O meu e-mail é...** _oo mehoo ee·mehl eh..._
Do you have a scanner?	**Tem um scanner?** _teng oong scanner_

Social Media

Are you on Facebook/Twitter?	**Está no Facebook/Twitter?** _ee·stah noo facebook/twitter_
What's your user name?	**Qual é o seu nome de utilizador?** _kwahl eh oo sehoo naum·eh deh oo·tee·lee·zuh·daur_
I'll add you as a friend.	**Vou adicioná-lo como amigo.** _vawoo·oo uh·dee·seeoo·nah·loo kau·moo uh·mee·goo_
I'll follow you on Twitter.	**Vou segui-lo no Twitter.** _vawoo·oo seh·gee·loo noo Twitter_
Are you following...?	**Está a seguir...?** _ee·stah uh seh·geer..._
I'll put the pictures on Facebook/Twitter.	**Vou colocar as fotos no Facebook/Twitter.** _vawoo koo·loo·khahr uhz faw·tawz noo Facebook/Twitter_
I'll tag you in the pictures.	**Vou identificá-lo nas fotos.** _vawoo ee·dehnt·tee·fee·kah·loo nuhz faw·tawz._

YOU MAY SEE...

FECHAR	close
APAGAR	delete
E-MAIL	e-mail
SAÍDA	exit
AJUDA	help
MESSENGER	instant messenger
INTERNET	internet
LOGIN	login
(NOVA) MENSAGEM	(new) message
LIGADO/DESLIGADO	on/off
ABRIR	open
IMPRIMIR [IMPRESSAR]	print
GUARDAR	save
ENVIAR	send
NOME DO UTILIZADOR [USUÁRIO]/SENHA	username/password
INTERNET WIRELESS	wireless internet

Phone

A phone card/prepaid phone, please.	**Um credifone/cartão de telefone pré-pago, por favor.** *oong kreh·dee·fawn/kuhr·tohm deh tehl·fawn preh·pah·goo poor fuh·vaur*
How much?	**Quanto é?** *kwuhn·too eh*
Where's the pay phone?	**Onde está o telefone pago?** *aund ee·stah oo tehl·fawn pah·goo*
My phone doesn't work here.	**O meu telefone não funciona aqui.** *oo meehoo tehl·fawn nohm foon·seeaw·nuh uh·kee*
What network are you on?	**Em que rede está?** *eng keh rreh·deh ee·stah*
Is it 3G?	**É 3G?** *eh trehz zseh*

I have run out of credit/ minutes.	**Fiquei sem crédito/minutos.** *fee·kay seng kreh·dee·too/mee·noo·tooz*
Can I buy some credit?	**Posso comprar algum crédito?** *paw·soo kaum·prahr ahl·goong kreh·dee·too?*
Do you have a phone charger?	**Tem um carregador de telefone?** *teng oong kah·rreh·guh·daur deh tehl·fawn*
What's the area/ country code for…?	**Qual é o código de área/país para…?** *kwahl eh oo kaw·dee·goo deh ah·eh·ree·uh/puh·eez puh·ruh…*
What's the number for Information?	**Qual é o número das Informações?** *kwahl eh oo noo·meh·roo duhz eeng·foor·muh·soingz*
I'd like the number for…	**Queria o número para…** *keh·ree·uh oo noo·meh·roo puh·ruh…*
I'd like to call collect [reverse the charges].	**Queria telefonar a cobrar no destino.** *keh·ree·uh tehl·fawn·ahr uh koo·brahr noo dehz·tee·noo*
Can I have your number?	**Pode dar-me o seu número de telefone?** *pawd dahr·meh oo sehoo noo·meh·roo deh tehl·fawn*
Here's my number.	**Este é o meu número.** *ehst eh oo mehoo noo·meh·roo*
Call me.	**Telefone-me.** *tehl·faw·neh·meh*
Text me.	**Manda-me uma mensagem de texto.** *muhn·duh·meh oo·muh mehn·sah·zseng deh tehk·stoo*
I'll call you.	**Eu ligo.** *eeoo lee·guh*
I'll text you.	**Mando-te uma mensagem de texto.** *muhn·doo·teh oo·muh mehn·sah·zseng deh tehk·stoo*

For Numbers, see page 173.

Telephone Etiquette

Hello. This is…	**Estou [Alô]. Fala…** *ee·stoo [ah·lawoo]. fah·luh…*
I'd like to speak to…	**Queria falar com…** *keh·ree·uh fuh·lahr kaum…*
Extension…	**Extensão…** *ehs·tehn·sohm…*
Speak louder/more slowly, please.	**Fale mais alto/devagar, por favor.** *fah·leh meyez ahl·too/deh·vuh·gahr poor fuh·vaur*

Could you repeat that?	**Importa-se de repetir?** *eeng·pawr·tuh·seh deh reh·peh·teer*
I'll call back later.	**Eu ligo mais tarde.** *eeoo lee·guh meyez tahrd*
Bye.	**Adeus.** *uh·deeooz*

For Business Travel, see page 147.

YOU MAY HEAR...

Quem fala? *keng fah·luh* — Who's calling?

Não desligue. *nohm dehs·lee·geh* — Hold on.

Vou-o ligar agora. *vauoo·oo lee·gahr uh·gaw·ruh* — I'll put you through.

Lamento, mas ele/ela não está. *luh·mehn·too muhz ehl/ehl·uh nohm ee·stah* — I'm afraid he's/she's not in.

Ele/Ela não pode atender o telefone. *ehl/ehl·uh nohm pawd uh·tehn·dehr oo tehl·fawn* — He/She can't come to the phone.

Quer deixar uma mensagem? *kehr day·shahr oo·muh mehn·sah·zseng* — Would you like to leave a message?

Ligue mais tarde/daqui dez minutos. *lee·geh meyez tahr·deh/da·kee·uh dehz mee·noo·tooz* — Call back later/in ten minutes.

Ele/Ela pode telefonar-lhe? *ehl/ehl·uh pawd tehl·fawn·ahr ly* — Can he/she call you back?

Qual é o seu número de telefone? *kwahl eh oo sehoo noo·meh·roo deh tehl·fawn* — What's your number?

Fax

| Can I send/receive a fax here? | **Posso enviar/receber um fax aqui?** *paw·soo ehn·vee·ahr/reh·seh·behr oong fahks uh·kee* |

What's the fax number?	**Qual é o número de fax?** *kwahl eh oo noo•meh•roo deh fahks*
Please fax this to…	**Por favor mande este fax para…** *poor fuh•vaur muhn•deh ehst fahks puh•ruh…*

There are over fifty thousand pay phones located throughout Portugal, operated by **PT Comunicações**. They are easy to use and offer different payment options with coins, phone cards, credit cards and ATM cards. Temporary mobile phones with 'pay as you go' plans are also available and may be more convenient. Internet cafes are increasingly popular to check e-mail and surf the net, and some public places do offer wireless internet access so that you can connect from your laptop.

Post

Where's the post office/mailbox [postbox]?	**Onde é que é o correio/a caixa do correio?** *aund eh keh eh oo koo•rray•oo/uh keye•shuh thoo koo•rray•oo*
A stamp for this postcard/letter, please.	**Um selo para este postal/esta carta, se faz favor.** *oong seh•loo puh•ruh ehst poo•stahl/eh•stuh kahr•tuh seh fahz fuh•vaur*
How much?	**Quanto é?** *kwuhn•too eh*
I want to send this package by airmail/express.	**Queria mandar este embrulho [pacote] por via aérea/correio expresso.** *keh•ree•uh muhn•dahr eh•stuh ehm•broo•lyoo [puh•kawt] poor vee•uh uh•eh•ree•uh/koo•rray•oo ees•preh•soo*
A receipt, please.	**Um recibo, se faz favor.** *oong reh•see•boo seh fahz fuh•vaur*

YOU MAY HEAR...

**Por favor preencha a declaração da
alfândega.** *poor fuh•vaur pree•ehn•shuh uh
deh•kluh•ruh•sohm duh uhl•fuhn•dee•guh*

Please fill out the customs
declaration form.

Qual é o valor? *kwahl eh oo vuh•laur*

What's the value?

O que é que tem dentro? *oo kee eh keh teng
dehn•troo*

What's inside?

Post offices in Portugal are indicated by signs reading CTT
(**Correios e Telecomunicações**). Hours are Monday–Friday
from 9:00 a.m. to 6:00 p.m.; main offices are also open on Saturday
and Sunday from 9:00 a.m. to 5:00 p.m. Red mailboxes are for **correio
normal** (normal mail) and blue for **correio azul** (express mail). You
can make phone calls at the post office; calls are paid for at the end of
the conversation. Stamps can be bought here or at any shop bearing
the sign of the red horse.

In Brazil, post offices bear the sign ECT (**Empresa Brasileira de
Correios e Telégrafos**); they are generally open from 8:00 a.m. to
6:00 p.m. Mondays through Fridays, and until noon on Saturdays.
Street corner mailboxes are yellow.

Food & Drink

ESSENTIAL

Can you recommend a good restaurant/bar?	**Pode recomendar-me um bom restaurante/bar?** *pawd reh•kaw•mehn•dahr•meh oong bohng reh•stahoo•ruhnt/bar*
Is there a(n) traditional Portuguese/ inexpensive restaurant near here?	**Há um restaurante tradicional português/ barato perto daqui?** *ah oong reh•stuhoo•ruhnt truh•dee•see•oo•nahl por•too•gehz/buh•rah•too pehr•too duh•kee*
A table for…, please.	**Uma mesa para…, se faz favor.** *oo•muh meh•zuh puh•ruh… seh fahz fuh•vaur*
Could we sit…?	**Podemos sentar-nos…?** *poo•deh•mooz sehn•tahr•nooz…*
here/there	**aqui/ali** *uh•kee/uh•lee*
outside	**lá fora** *lah faw•ruh*
in a non-smoking area	**na área para não-fumadores [não-fumantes]** *nuh ah•ree•uh puh•ruh nohmfoo•muh•daur•ehs [nohmfoo•muhnts]*
I'm waiting for someone.	**Estou à espera de alguém.** *ee•stawoo ah ee•speh•ruh deh ahl•gehm*
Where's the restroom [toilet]?	**Onde são as casas de banho [os banheiros]?** *aund sohmuhz kah•zuhz deh buh•nyoo [ooz buh•nyay•rooz]*
A menu, please.	**Uma ementa, por favor.** *oo•muh ee•mehn•tuh poor fuh•vaur*
What do you recommend?	**O que é que me recomenda?** *oo keh eh keh meh reh•koo•mehn•duh*
I'd like…	**Queria…** *keh•ree•uh…*

Some more..., please. **Mais..., se faz favor.** *meyez...seh fahz fuh•vaur*

Enjoy your meal. **Bom apetite.** *bohng uh•peh•tee•teh*

The check [bill], please. **A conta, por favor.** *uh kaum•tuh poor fuh•vaur*

Is service included? **O serviço está incluído?** *oo sehr•vee•soo ee•stah een•kloo•ee•thoo*

Can I pay by credit card? **Posso pagar com cartão de crédito?** *paw•soo puh•gahr kaumkuhr•tohm deh kreh•dee•too*

Could I have a receipt, please? **Pode darme uma factura [um recibo], por favor?** *pawd dahr•meh oo•muh fah•too•ruh [oong reh•see•boo] poor fuh•vaur*

Thank you. **Obrigado** *m* /**Obrigada** *f*. *aw•bree•gah•thoo/ aw•bree•gah•thuh*

Where to Eat

Can you recommend...? **Pode recomendar-me...?** *pawd reh•koo•mehn•dahr•meh...*

    a restaurant **um restaurante** *oong reh•stuhoo•ruhnt*

    a bar **um bar** *oong bar*

    a cafe **um café** *oong kuh•feh*

a fast-food place	**um restaurante de comida rápida [uma cadeia de fast food]** oong reh·stuhoo·<u>ruhnt</u> deh koo·<u>mee</u>·duh <u>rah</u>·pee·duh [<u>oo</u>·muh kuh·<u>day</u>·uh deh fast food]
a seafood restaurant	**uma marisqueira [um restaurante de frutos do mar]** <u>oo</u>·muh muh·ree·<u>skay</u>·ruh [oong reh·stuhoo·<u>ruhnt</u> deh <u>froo</u>·tooz doo mahr]
a cheap restaurant	**um restaurante barato** oong rehz·tahoo·ruhnt buh·<u>rah</u>·too
an expensive resturant	**um restaurante caro** oong rehz·tahoo·ruhnt <u>kah</u>·roo
a restaurant with a good view	**um restaurante com boa vista** oong rehz·tahoo·ruhnt kaum bau·uh vee·stuh
an authentic/non-touristy restaurant	**um restaurante típico/não turístico** oong rehz·tahoo·ruhnt <u>tee</u>·pee·koo/nohm too·ree·<u>stee</u>·koo

Reservations & Preferences

I'd like to reserve a table…	**Queria reservar uma mesa…** keh·<u>ree</u>·uh reh·zehr·<u>vahr</u> <u>oo</u>·muh <u>meh</u>·zuh…
for two	**para dois** <u>puh</u>·ruh doyz
for this evening	**para hoje à noite** <u>puh</u>·ruh auzseh ah noyt
for tomorrow at…	**para amanhã às…** <u>puh</u>·ruh uh·muh·<u>nyuh</u> ahz…
A table for two.	**Uma mesa para dois.** <u>oo</u>·muh <u>meh</u>·zuh <u>puh</u>·ruh doyz
We have a reservation.	**Temos uma reserva.** <u>teh</u>·mooz <u>oo</u>·muh reh·<u>zehr</u>·vuh
My name is…	**Chamo-me… [Meu nome é…]** <u>shuh</u>·moo·meh… [mehoo <u>naum</u>·ee eh…]
Could we sit…?	**Podemos sentar-nos…?** poo·<u>deh</u>·mooz sehn·<u>tahr</u>·nooz…
here/there	**aqui/ali** uh·<u>kee</u>/uh·<u>lee</u>
outside	**lá fora** lah <u>faw</u>·ruh

in a non-smoking area	**na área para não-fumadores [não-fumantes]** *nuh ah•ree•uh puh•ruh nohmfoo•muh•daur•ehs [nohmfoo•muhnts]*
by the window	**à janela** *ah zsuh•neh•luh*
in the shade	**à sombra** *ah sohng•bruh*
in the sun	**ao sol** *ahoo sawl*
Where are the restrooms [toilets]?	**Onde são as casas de banho [os banheiros]?** *aund sohmuhz kah•zuhz deh buh•nyoo [ooz buh•nyay•rooz]*

YOU MAY HEAR...

Tem reserva? *teng reh•sehr•vuh*	Do you have a reservation?
Quantas pessoas? *kwuhn•tuhz peh•sau•uhs*	How many?
Fumador ou não-fumador [fumante ou não-fumante]? *foo•muh•daur aw nohmfoo•muh•daur [foo•muhnt aw nohmfoo•muhnt]*	Smoking or non-smoking?
Deseja encomendar? *deh•zeh•zsuh ehn•caw•mehn•dahr*	Would you like to order?
O que deseja? *oo keh deh•zeh•zsuh*	What would you like?
Recomendo... *reh•koo•mehn•doo...*	I recommend...
Bom apetite. *bohng uh•peh•tee•teh*	Enjoy your meal.

How to Order

Excuse me!	**Se faz favor!** *seh fahz fuh•vaur*
We're ready to order.	**Estamos prontos para encomendar.** *ee•stuh•mooz prawn•tooz puh•ruh eng•kau•mehn•dahr*

The wine list, please.	**A carta dos vinhos, se faz favor.** *uh kahr•tuh dooz vee•nyooz seh fahz fuh•vaur*
I'd like…	**Queria…** *keh•ree•uh…*
a bottle of…	**uma garrafa…** *oo•muh guh•rrah•fuh…*
a carafe of…	**um jarro de…** *oomjah•rroo deh…*
a glass of…	**um copo de…** *oong kaw•poo deh…*
A menu, please.	**Uma ementa, por favor.** *oo•muh ee•mehn•tuh poor fuh•vaur*
Do you have…?	**Tem…?** *teng…*
a menu in English	**uma ementa em Inglês** *oo•muh ee•mehn•tuh eng een•glehz*
a fixed-price menu	**uma ementa de preço-fixo** *oo•muh ee•mehn•tuh deh preh•soo feek•soo*
a children's menu	**uma ementa de criança** *oo•muh ee•mehn•tuh deh kree•uhn•suh*
What do you recommend?	**O que é que me recomenda?** *oo kee eh keh meh reh•koo•mehn•duh*
What's this?	**O que é isto?** *oo kee eh ee•stoo*
What's in it?	**Leva o quê?** *leh•vuh oo keh*
Is it spicy?	**É picante?** *eh pee•kuhnt*
I'd like…	**Queria…** *keh•ree•uh…*
More…, please.	**Mais…, se faz favor.** *meyez… seh fahz fuh•vaur*
With/Without…	**Com/Sem…** *kaum/seng…*
I can't have…	**Não posso ter…** *nohmpaw•soo tehr…*
rare	**mal passado** *m* **/passada** *f mahl puh•sah•thoo/ puh•sah•thuh*
medium	**meio passado** *m* **/passada** *f may•oo puh•sah•thoo/ puh•sah•thuh*
well-done	**bem passado** *m* **/passada** *f beng puh•sah•thoo/ puh•sah•thuh*
It's to go [take away].	**É para levar.** *eh puh•ruh leh•vahr*

YOU MAY SEE...

COUVERT	cover charge
PREÇO-FIXO	fixed-price
EMENTA	menu
UMA EMENTA DO DIA	menu of the day
SERVIÇO (NÃO) INCLUÍDO	service (not) included
ESPECIAIS	specials

Cooking Methods

baked	**alourado** m /**alourada** f [**dourado** m / **dourada** f] uh·lauoo·_rah_·thoo/uh·lauoo·_rah_·thuh [dauoo·_rah_·doo/dauoo·_rah_·duh]
boiled	**cozido** m /**cozida** f koo·_zee_·thoo/koo·_zee_·thuh
braised	**estufado** m /**estufada** f ee·stoo·_fah_·thoo/ ee·stoo·_fah_·thuh
breaded	**panado** m /**panada** f [**empanado** m /**empanada** f] puh·_nah_·thoo/puh·_nah_·thuh [ehm·puh·_nah_·doo/ ehm·puh·_nah_·dah]
creamed	**com natas** kohng _nah_·tuhz
diced	**aos cubos** ahooz _koo_·booz
filet of...	**filete de...** fee·_leht_ deh...
fried	**frito** m /**frita** f _free_·too/_free_·tuh
grilled	**grelhado** m /**grelhada** f gree·_lyah_·thoo/ gree·_lyah_·thuh
poached	**escalfado** m /**escalfada** f ees·kahl·_fah_·thoo/ ees·kahl·_fah_·thuh
roasted	**assado** m /**assada** f uh·_sah_·thoo/uh·_sah_·thuh
sautéed	**salteado** m /**salteada** f sahl·tee·_ah_·thoo/ sahl·tee·_ah_·thuh

smoked	**fumado** m /**fumada** f [**defumado** m /**defumada** f] foo·*mah*·thoo/foo·*mah*·thuh [deh·foo·*mah*·doo/ deh·foo·*mah*·duh]
steamed	**cozido** m /**cozida** f **a vapor** koo·*zee*·thoo/ koo·*zee*·thuh uh vuh·*paur*
stewed	**guisado** m /**guisada** f [**ensopado** m /**ensopada** f] gee·*zah*·thoo/gee·*zah*·thuh [een·soo·*pah*·doo/ een·soo·*pah*·duh]
stuffed	**recheado** m /**recheada** f reh·shee·*ah*·thoo/ reh·shee·*ah*·thuh

Dietary Requirements

I am...	**Sou...** sauoo...
diabetic	**diabético** m /**diabética** f dee·uh·*beh*·tee·koo/ dee·uh·*beh*·tee·kuh
lactose intolerant	**intolerante à lactose** een·tawl·eh·*ruhnt* ah *lahk*·tawz
vegetarian	**vegetariano** m /**vegetariana** f veh·zseh·tuh·ree·*uh*·noo/veh·zseh·tuh·ree·*uh*·nuh
vegan	**vegetariano** veh·geh·tuh·ree·uh·noo
I'm allergic to...	**Sou alérgico** m /**alérgica** f **a...** sauoo uh·*lehr*·gee·koo/uh·*lehr*·gee·kuh uh...
I can't eat...	**Não posso comer...** nohm *paw*·soo koo·*mehr*...
dairy	**lacticínios** lahk·tee·*see*·nee·ooz
gluten	**glúten** gloo·*tehn*
nuts	**nozes** *naw*·zehz
pork	**carne de porco** *kahrr*·neh deh *paur*·koo
shellfish	**marisco** muh·*ree*·skoo
spicy foods	**comidas picantes** koo·*mee*·duhz pee·*kuhnts*
wheat	**trigo** *tree*·goo
Is it halal/kosher?	**É halal/kosher?** eh uh·*lahl*/*kaw*·shehr

Do you have...?	**Tem...?** teng...
skimmed milk	**leite magro** layt mah·groo
whole milk	**leite gordo** layt goahr·doo
soya milk	**leite de soja** layt deh saw·zsuh

Dining with Children

Do you have children's portions?
Tem doses [porções] para crianças? teng <u>daw</u>·zer [poor·<u>soings</u>] puh·ruh kree·<u>uhn</u>·suhz

A child's seat, please.
Um assento de criança, por favor. oong uh·<u>sehn</u>·too deh kree·<u>uhn</u>·suh poor fuh·<u>vaur</u>

Can I have a highchair/child's seat?
Tem uma cadeira alta/cadeirinha de criança? teng oo·muh kuh·<u>day</u>·ruh ahl·tuh/kuh·<u>day</u>·ree·nyuh deh kree·<u>uhn</u>·suh

Where can I feed/change the baby?
Onde posso alimentar/mudar o bebé [neném]? aund <u>paw</u>·soo uh·lee·mehn·<u>tahr</u>/moo·<u>dahr</u> oo beh·beh [neh·<u>neh</u>]

Can you warm this?
Pode aquecer isto? pawd uh·keh·<u>sehr</u> ee·stoo

For Traveling with Children, see page 150.

How to Complain

How much longer will our food be?
Quanto tempo demora a nossa comida? <u>kwuhn</u>·too <u>tehm</u>·poo deh·<u>maw</u>·ruh uh <u>naw</u>·suh koo·<u>mee</u>·thuh

We can't wait any longer.
Não podemos esperar mais. nohm poo·<u>deh</u>·mooz ee·speh·<u>rahr</u> meyez

We're leaving.
Vamo-nos embora. <u>vuh</u>·moo·nooz ehm·<u>baw</u>·ruh

I didn't order this.
Não encomendei isso. nohm ehn·koo·mehn·<u>day</u> ee·soo

I ordered...
Encomendei... ehn·koo·mehn·<u>day</u>...

I can't eat this.
Não posso comer isto. nohm <u>paw</u>·soo koo·<u>mehr</u> ee·stoo

This is too...	**Isto está muito...**	*ee-stoo ee-stah mooee-too...*
cold/hot	**frio/quente**	*free-oo/kehnt*
salty/spicy	**salgado/picante**	*sahl-gah-thoo/pee-kuhnt*
tough/bland	**duro/insosso**	*doo-roo/een-saw-soo*
This isn't clean/fresh.	**Isto não está limpo/fresco.**	*ee-stoo nohm ee-stah leem-poo/frehs-koo*

Paying

The check [bill], please.	**A conta, por favor.**	*uh kaum-tuh poor fuh-vaur*
Separate checks [bills], please.	**Contas separadas, por favor.**	*kaum-tuhz seh-puh-rah-duhz poor fuh-vaur*
It's all together.	**É tudo junto.**	*eh too-doo zsoon-too*
Is service included?	**O serviço está incluído?**	*oo sehr-vee-soo ee-stah een-kloo-ee-thoo*
What's this amount for?	**De que é este valor?**	*deh keh eh eh-stuh vuh-loahr*
I didn't have that. I had...	**Eu não comi isso. Eu comi...**	*ehoo nohm koo-mee ee-soo. ehoo koo-mee...*
Can I pay by credit card?	**Posso pagar com cartão de crédito?**	*paw-soo puh-gahr kaum kuhr-tohm deh kreh-dee-too*
Can I have an itemized bill/a receipt?	**Pode dar-me uma conta detalhada/uma factura [um recibo]?**	*pawd dahr-meh oo-muh kaum-tuh deh-tuh-lyah-duh/oo-muh fah-too-ruh [oong reh-see-boo]*

Portuguese food is inspired by its location off the Atlantic Ocean; much of its cuisine is comprised of fish, especially salted cod. Typical Portuguese food is often the simple, delicious fare of fisherman and farmers. Expect to find fish, meat, rice and potatoes combined with olive oil and wine. Restaurant owners and wait staff are generally extremely friendly.

| That was a very good meal. | **Foi uma refeição excelente.** *foy <u>oo</u>•muh reh•fay•<u>sohm</u> eh•seh•<u>lehnt</u>* |
| I've already paid. | **Já paguei.** *zsah puh•gay.* |

O pequeno almoço

Breakfast (known as **café da manhã** in Brazil) is usually served from 7:00 to 10:00 a.m. In Portugal it is comprised of coffee, rolls, butter and jam. In Brazil, the addition of fresh fruit juice, fruit, toast and pastry makes for a heartier meal.

O almoço

Lunch is the main meal of the day, served from12:30 to 2:30 p.m. Shops are normally closed during these hours. In Brazilian resorts, lunch is often served without interruption from12:30 till evening. It generally includes soup or salad, fish or meat, and a dessert.

O jantar

Dinner is served fromabout 7:30 to 10:00 p.m., except in a Portuguese **casa de fado** ('house of blues' dinner theater), where dinner is served a bit later. In Brazil dinner is from 8:00 to 11:00 p.m. Dinner typically includes soup, fish or meat, salad, bread, and fruit or a sweet for dessert. Coffee or espresso is almost always served at the end of every meal.

Breakfast

a água *uh ah-gwuh*	water
o bolinho *oo bau-lee-nyoo*	muffin
o café.../chá... *oo kuh-feh.../shah...*	coffee.../tea...
com açúcar *kaum uh-soo-kuhr*	with sugar
com adoçante artificial *kaum uh-thoo-suhnt uhr-tee-fee-see-ahl*	with artificial sweetner
com leite *kaum layt*	with milk
descafeínado *dehz-kuh-fay-nah-thoo*	decaf
bica [cafezinho] *bee-kuh [kuh-feh-zee-nyoo]*	black
as carnes frias *uhz kahr-nehz free-uhz*	cold cuts [charcuterie]
o cereal (frio/quente) *oo seh-ree-ahl (free-oo/kehnt)*	(cold/hot) cereal
o doce de fruta [geleia] *oo dau-seh deh froo-tuh [zseh-lay-uh]*	jam
a farinha de aveia *uh fuh-ree-nyuh deh uh-vay-uh*	oatmeal
o leite *oo layt*	milk
a manteiga *uh muhn-tay-guh*	butter
a omelete *uh aw-meh-leh-tuh*	omelet
o iogurte *uh yaw-goort*	yogurt
o ovo... *oo au-voo...*	...egg
muito fervido/fervido macio *mooee-too fehr-vee-thoo/fehr-vee-thoo muh-see-oo*	hard-boiled/ soft-boiled
estrelado [frito] *ee-struh-lah-doo [free-too]*	fried
mexido *meh-shee-doo*	scrambled
o pão *oo pohm*	bread
o papo-seco [pãozinho] *oo pah-poo seh-koo [pohm-zee-nyoo]*	roll

o queijo *oo kay·zsoo*	cheese
as salsichas *uhz sahl·see·shuhz*	sausages
o sumo [suco] de... *oo soo·moo [soo·koo] deh*	...juice
fruta *froo·tuh*	fruit
maçã *muh·suh*	apple
toranja *uh taw·ruhn·zsuh*	grapefruit
laranja *luh·ruhn·zsuh*	orange
o toucinho *oo taw·see·nyoo*	bacon
as torradas *uhz too·rrah·duhz*	toast
o yogurte *oo yaw·goort*	yogurt

Appetizers

as carnes frias *uhz kahr·nehz free·uhz*	cold cuts
o chouriço *oo shauoo·ree·soo*	sausage
as lulas à milanesa *uhz loo·luhz ah mee·luh·neh·zuh*	squid
o paio *oo peye·oo*	smoked pork fillet (Port.)
os pimentos assados *ooz pee·mehn·tooz uh·sah·dooz*	roasted peppers
o pipis *oo pee·peez*	spicy chicken stew
a santola recheada *uh suhn·taw·luh eh·shee·ah·thuh*	stuffed crab

Soup

o caldo verde *oo kahl·doo vehrd*	potato and kale soup with sausage
o gaspacho *oo guhz·pah·shoo*	chilled soup with tomatoes, sweet peppers, onions, cucumbers and croutons
as migas de bacalhau *uhz mee·guhz deh buh·kuh·lyahoo*	dried cod soup with garlic and bread

a sopa açorda à Alentejana *a sau·puh uh·saur·duh ah uh·luhn·teh·zsuh·nuh* — bread soup with garlic and herbs

a sopa de cozido *a sau·puh deh koo·zee·doo* — meat broth with vegetables and macaroni

a sopa seca *uh sau·puh seh·kuh* — thick soup with meat, cabbage and bread

a sopa transmontana *a sau·puh truhnz·moo·tuh·nuh* — vegetable soup with bacon and bread

a sopa... *uh sau·puh...* — ...soup

   à pescador *ah pehs·kuh·daur* — fish

   canja *keng·zsuh* — chicken and rice

   de abóbora *deh uh·baw·buh·ruh* — pumpkin

   de agriões *deh uh·gree·oings* — potato and watercress

   de coentros *deh koo·eng·trooz* — coriander, bread, and poached eggs

   de ervilhas *deh eer·vee·lyuhz* — green pea

Fish & Seafood

o atum *oo uh·toong* — tuna

as amêijoas à Bulhão Pato *uhz uh·may·zsoo·uhz ah boo·lyohm pah·too* — clams with coriander, garlic and onion

as amêijoas à Portuguesa *uhz uh·may·zsoo·uhz ah poor·too·geh·zuh* — clams with garlic, parsley and olive oil

o bacalhau à Gomes de Sá *oo buh·kuh·lyahoo ah gau·mehz deh sah* — dried cod with olives, garlic, onions, parsley and hard-boiled eggs

o bacalhau podre *oo buh·kuh·lyahoo pau·dreh* — baked layers of cod and fried potatoes

a cabeça de pescada cozida *uh kuh·beh·suh deh peh·skah·thuh koo·zee·thuh* — fish stew

os camarões... *ooz kuh·muh·roings...* — ...shrimp [prawns]

   fritos *free·tooz* — fried

grandes _gruhn·dehz_	large [king] (Braz.)
no espeto _noo ee·speh·too_	on a stick (Braz.)
a caldeirada… _uh kahl·day·rah·thuh…_	fish with onions, tomatoes, potatoes, olive oil…
à fragateira _ah fruh·guh·tay·ruh_	shellfish and mussels in a fish stock with tomatoes
à moda da Póvoa _ah maw·duh duh praw·voo·uh_	hake, skate, sea bass and eel
o espadarte _oo ees·puh·dahrt_	swordfish
a lagosta _uh luh·gau·stuh_	lobster
a lampreia _uh luhm·pray·uh_	lamprey
o linguado _oo leeng·gwah·thoo_	sole
as lulas _uhz loo·luhz_	squid
as lulas recheadas _uhz loo·luhz reh·shee·ah·duhz_	stuffed squid
os mariscos _ooz muh·rees·kooz_	seafood
a moqueca de peixe _uh moo·keh·kuh deh paysh_	stew made of fish, shellfish or shrimp with coconut milk (Braz.)
as ostras do Algarve _uhz aw·struhz thoo ahl·gahrv_	oysters in butter and wine (Algarve)
o pargo _oo pahr·goo_	bream
o polvo _oo paul·voo_	octopus
o vatapá _oo vuh·tuh·pah_	fish and shrimp in a paste made of flour or breadcrumbs (Braz.)

Meat & Poultry

o arroz de frango _oo uh·rrauz deh fruhn·goo_	chicken with white wine, hamand rice
o bife [filete] _oo beef [fee·leh·chee]_	steak

o bife na frigideira *oo beef nuh free•zsuh•day•ruh* — steak fried in butter, white wine and garlic

o borrego [carneiro] *oo boo•rreh•goo [kuhr•nay•roo]* — lamb

a carne de porco *uh kahrn deh paur•koo* — pork

a carne de sol com feijão verde *uh kahrn deh sol kaum fay•zsohm vehrd* — sun-dried meat (jerky) with green beans (Braz.)

a carne de vaca *uh kahrn deh vah•kuh* — beef

o carneiro guisado [ensopado] *oo kuhrr•nay•roo gee•zah•thoo [eng•soo•pah•do]* — mutton with tomatoes, garlic and herbs

o coelho *oo koo•eh•lyoo* — rabbit

a costeleta *uh koo•stuh•leh•tuh* — cutlet

o cozido à Portuguesa *oo koo•zee•doo ah poor•too•geh•zuh* — boiled beef, bacon, smoked sausage and vegetables

a feijoada *uh fay•zsoo•ah•duh* — Brazil's national dish: black beans cooked with bacon, salted pork, jerky and sausage

o frango *oo fruhn•goo* — chicken

o frango na púcara *oo fruhn•goo nuh poo•keh•ruh* — chicken stewed in port and cognac, then fried with almonds

o medalhão *uh meh•duh•lyohm* — tenderloin steak

a perdiz à caçador *oo pehr•deez uh kuh•suh•daur* — partridge simmered with carrots, onions, white wine and herbs

o presunto *oo preh•zoon•too* — cured ham

as tripas à moda do Porto *uhz tree•puhz ah maw•duh thoo paur•too* — tripe cooked with pork, beans and chicken

a vitela *uh vee•tehl•uh* — veal

o xinxim de galinha *oo sheeng·sheeng deh guh·lee·nyuh* chicken cooked in dried shrimp, peanuts and parsley (Braz.)

In Portugal, many dishes are served with both rice and potatoes. Almost every meal is served with a salad. Portugal is not a very vegetarian-friendly country, and vegetarians may have a difficult time finding meals in restaurants outside of Lisbon, Porto or the Algarve.

Vegetables & Staples

o açafrão *oo uh·suh·frohm*	saffron
o acarajé *oo uh·kuh·ruh·zseh*	grated beans fried in palmoil, served with pepper sauce, onions and shrimp (Braz.)
o açúcar *oo uh·soo·kuhr*	sugar
as alcaparras *uhz ahl·kuh·pah·rruhz*	capers
a alface *uh ahl·fah·seh*	lettuce
as amêndoas *uhz uh·mehn·doo·uhz*	almonds
o arroz... *oo uh·rrauz...*	rice...
de alhos *deh ah·lyooz*	with garlic
de cozido *deh koo·zee·thoo*	cooked in meat stock
de feijão *de fay·zsohm*	with beans
as batatas... *uhz buh·tah·tuhz...*	potatoes...
cozidas *koo·zee·duhz*	boiled
cozidas com pele *koo·zee·duhz kohm pehl*	boiled in their skins
fritas *free·tuhz*	fries [chips]
de palha *deh pah·lyuh*	matchsticks
o puré de batatas *oo poo·reh deh buh·tah·tuhz*	mashed potatoes

as cebolas *uhz seh·bau·luhz*	onions
os cogumelos *ooz koo·goo·meh·looz*	mushrooms
as ervilhas *uhz eer·vee·lyuhz*	peas
a farinha *uh fuh·ree·nyuh*	flour
as favas *uhz fah·vuhz*	broad beans
o feijão *oo fay·zsohm*	kidney beans
o feijão verde *oo fay·zsohm vehrd*	green beans
o manjericão *oo muhn·zseh·ree·kohm*	basil
a manteiga *uh muhn·tay·guh*	butter
as massas *uhz mah·suhz*	pasta
o pão *oo pohm*	bread
os pimentos *ooz pee·mehn·tooz*	peppers
o rutu à mineira *oo rroo·too ah mee·nay·ruh*	beans, cassava, flour, pork, cabbage, fried eggs and bacon (Braz.)
a salsa *uh sahl·suh*	parsley

Fruit

o abacate *oo uh·buh·kaht*	avocado
o abacaxi *oo uh·buh·kah·shee*	pineapple
os alperces *ooz uhl·pehr·sehz*	apricots
as ameixas *uhz uh·may·shuhz*	plums
o arando *oo uh·ruhn·doo*	cranberry
a banana *uh buh·nuh·nuh*	banana
as cerejas *uhz seh·ray·zsuhz*	cherries
o coco *oo kaw·koo*	coconut
a framboesa *uh fruhm·booeh·zuh*	raspberry
a fruta *uh froo·tuh*	fruit
a goiaba *uh goy·ah·buh*	guava
o kiwi *oo kee·wee*	kiwi
a laranja *uh luh·ruhn·zsuh*	orange

a lima *uh lee·muh*	lime
o limão *oo lee·mohm*	lemon
a maçã *uh muh·suh*	apple
o mamão *oo muh·mohm*	papaya
a manga *uh muhn·guh*	mango
a mexerica *uh meh·sheh·ree·kuh*	tangerine
a melancia *uh muh·luhn·see·uh*	watermelon
o melão *oo meh·lohm*	melon
o mirtilo *oo meer·tee·loo*	blueberry
os morangos *ooz moo·ruhn·gooz*	strawberries
a pêra *uh peh·ruh*	pear
o pêssego *oo pay·seh·goo*	peach
a toranja *uh taw·ruhn·zsa*	grapefruit
as uvas *uhz oo·vuhz*	grapes

Cheese

o azeitão *oo uh·zay·tohm*	creamy cheese
a bola *uh bau·luh*	hard cow's milk cheese
o cabreiro *oo kuh·bray·roo*	goat's milk cheese
o castelo branco *oo kuh·steh·loo bruhn·koo*	creamy blue cheese
a évora *uh eh·voo·ruh*	creamy cheese
a ilha *uh ee·lyuh*	cow's milk cheese from the Azores Islands (Port.)
o queijo *oo kay·zsoo*	cheese
o queijo de Minas *oo·kay·zsoo deh mee·nuhz*	Brazilian cow's milk cheese
o requeijão *oo reh·kay·zsohm*	creamy Brazilian cheese
o serra *oo she·rruh*	creamy goat's milk cheese
macio *muh·see·oo*	soft
duro *doo·roo*	hard
suave *swahv*	mild
forte *fawrt*	strong

Dessert

a arrufada de Coimbra *uh uh·rroo·fah·duh deh kooeem·bruh*	cinnamon dough cake
a babá-de-moça *uh buh·bah deh mau·suh*	dessert made of egg yolk, coconut milk and syrup (Braz.)
o bolo podre *oo bau·loo pau·dreh*	honey and cinnamon cake
as broas castelares *uhz brau·uhz kuh·steh·lah·rehz*	sweet-potato biscuits
a canjica *uh kuhn·zsee·kuh*	dessert made with sweet corn and milk (Braz.)
a goiabada *uh goy·uh·bah·duh*	thick paste made of guavas (Braz.)
a mousse de maracujá *uh moo·seh deh muh·ruh·koo·zsah*	passion fruit mousse (Braz.)
os ovos moles de Aveiro *ooz aw·vooz mawlz deh ah·vay·roo*	egg yolks cooked in syrup
o pastel de Tentúgal *oo puhz·tehl deh tehn·too·gahl*	pastry filled with egg yolks cooked in syrup
pudim flan *poo·deeng fluhn*	caramel custard
quindim *keeng·deeng*	coconut and egg yolk pudding (Braz.)

Sauces & Condiments

o sal *o sahl*	salt
a pimenta *uh pee·mehn·tuh*	pepper
mostarda *mooz·tahr·duh*	mustard
ketchup *ketchup*	ketchup

At the Market

Where are the trolleys/ baskets?	**Onde estão os carrinhos/cestos?** *aund ee·stohm ooz kuh·rree·nyooz/sehs·tooz*

Where is…?	**Onde é…?**	aund eh…
I'd like some of that/those.	**Queria disso/desses.**	keh·<u>ree</u>·uh <u>thee</u>·soo/<u>theh</u>·seh
Can I taste it?	**Posso provar?**	<u>paw</u>·soo proo·<u>vahr</u>
I'd like…	**Queria…**	keh·<u>ree</u>·uh…
a kilo/half-kilo of…	**um quilo/meio quilo de…**	oong <u>kee</u>·loo/<u>may</u>·oo <u>kee</u>·loo deh…
a liter/half-liter of…	**um litro/meio litro de…**	oong <u>lee</u>·troo/<u>may</u>·oo <u>lee</u>·troo deh…
I'd like…	**Queria…**	keh·<u>ree</u>·uh…
a piece of…	**uma fatia de…**	<u>oo</u>·muh fuh·<u>tee</u>·uh deh…
a slice of…	**um pedaço de…**	oong peh·<u>dah</u>·soo deh…
More./Less.	**Mais./Menos.**	meyez/<u>meh</u>·nooz
How much?	**Quanto é?**	<u>kwuhn</u>·too eh
Where do I pay?	**Onde pago?**	aund <u>pah</u>·goo
A bag, please.	**Un saco, por favor.**	oong <u>sah</u>·koo poor fuh·<u>vaur</u>
I'm being helped.	**Alguém está a ajudar-me.**	ahl·<u>geng</u> ee·<u>stah</u> uh uh·zsoo·<u>dahr</u>·meh

For Conversion Tables, see page 178.

YOU MAY HEAR…

Deseja alguma coisa? deh·<u>zeh</u>·zsuh ahl·<u>goo</u>·muh coy·zuh	Would you like something?
O que é que deseja? oo kee eh keh deh·<u>zeh</u>·zsuh	What would you like?
Mais alguma coisa? meyez ahl·<u>goo</u>·muh <u>coy</u>·zuh	Anything else?
São…euros. sohm…<u>ehoo</u>·rooz	That's…euros.

Street markets are an integral part of Portuguese life, but you must get there early to get the full experience. By 10:00 a.m. the best things are gone. Most markets are held in the town square on a weekly basis. Everything can be found here, from quality food, antiques and handicrafts to household items and clothes. Larger towns and cities may have covered markets that are open Monday through Saturday where you can buy fresh fish, meat, fruit and vegetables. Portuguese cheese, both delicious and inexpensive, is one of the most popular items at any market.

YOU MAY SEE...

USAR ATÉ...	best if used by...
CALORIAS	calories
SEM GORDURA	fat free
MANTER NO FRIO	keep refrigerated
PODE CONTER VESTÍGIOS DE...	may contain traces of...
MICROONDAS	microwaveable
DATA DE VENDA...	sell by...
PRÓPRIO PARA VEGETARIANOS	suitable for vegetarians

In the Kitchen

bottle opener	**o abre-garrafas [abridor de garrafas]** *oo ah·breh guh·rrah·fuhz [uh·bree·daur deh guh·rrah·fuhz]*
bowl	**a malga** *uh mahl·guh*
can opener	**o abre-latas [abridor de latas]** *oo ah·breh lah·tuhz [ah·bree·daur deh lah·tuhz]*
corkscrew	**o saca-rolhas** *oo sah·kuh rau·lyuhz*

cups	**as chávenas [xícaras]** *uhz shah•vee•nuhz [shee•kuh•ruhz]*
forks	**os garfos** *ooz gahr•fooz*
frying pan	**a frigideira** *uh free•zsee•thay•ruh*
glasses	**os copos** *ooz kaw•pooz*
knife	**as facas** *uhz fah•kuhz*
measuring cup/spoon	**o copo/a colher de medir** *oo kaw•poo/uh koo•lyehr deh meh•deer*
paper napkin	**o guardanapo de papel** *oo gwahr•duh•nah•poo deh puh•pehl*
plates	**os pratos** *ooz prah•tooz*
pot	**a panela** *uh puh•neh•luh*
saucepan	**o tacho [a caçarola]** *oo tah•shoo [uh kuh•suh•rawl•uh]*
spatula	**a espátula** *uh ees•pah•too•luh*
spoon	**as colheres** *uhz koo•lyeh•rehz*

Drinks

ESSENTIAL

The wine list/drink menu, please.	**A carta dos vinhos/ementa de bebidas, se faz favor.** *uh kahr•tuh dooz vee•nyooz/ee•mehn•tuh deh beh•bee•duhz seh fahz fuh•vaur*
What do you recommend?	**O que é que me recomenda?** *oo keh eh keh meh reh•koo•mehn•düh*
I'd like a bottle/glass of red/white wine.	**Queria uma garrafa/um copo de vinho tinto/branco.** *keh•ree•uh oo•muh guh•rrah•fuh/oong kaw•poo deh vee•nyoo teen•too/bruhn•koo*

The house wine, please.	**O vinho da casa, se faz favor.** *oo vee·nyoo duh kah·zuh seh fahz fuh·vaur*
Another bottle/glass, please.	**Outra garrafa/Outro copo, se faz favor.** *auoo·truh guh·rrah·fuh/auoo·troo kaw·poo ser fahz fuh·vaur*
I'd like a local beer.	**Gostaria uma cerveja local.** *goo·stuh·ree·uh oo·muh sehr·vay·zsuh loo·kahl*
Can I buy you a drink?	**Posso oferecer-lhe uma bebida?** *paw·soo aw·freh·sehr·lyeh oo·muh beh·bee·thuh*
Cheers!	**Viva!** *vee·vuh*
A coffee/tea, please.	**Um café/chá, se faz favor.** *oong kuh·feh/shah seh fahz fuh·vaur*
Black.	**Bica [Cafezinho].** *bee·kuh [kuh·feh·zee·nyoo]*
With…	**com…** *kaum…*
milk	**leite** *layt*
sugar	**açúcar** *uh·soo·kuhr*
artificial sweetener	**adoçante** *uh·doo·suhnty*
A…, please.	**…, se faz favor.** *…seh fahz fuh·vaur*
juice	**Um sumo [suco]** *oong soo·moo [soo·koo]*
soda	**Um refresco** *oong reh·freh·skoo*
sparkling/still	**Uma água com/sem gás** *oo·muh ah·gwuh*
water	*kaum/sehmgahz*
Is the tap water safe to drink?	**A água da torneira é boa para beber?** *uh ah·gwuh duh toor·nay·ruh eh baw·uh puh·ruh beh·behr*

Non-alcoholic Drinks

a água de coco *uh ah·gwuh deh kau·koo*	coconut juice (Braz.)
a água com/sem gás *uh ah·gwuh kaum/ sehn gahz*	carbonated/noncarbonated [still] water
o chá frio *oo shah free·oo*	iced tea
o café *oo kuh·feh*	coffee

o caldo de cana *oo kahl·doo deh kuh·nuh*	sugar-cane juice (Braz.)
o leite *oo layt*	milk
o leite de coco *oo layt deh kau·koo*	coconut milk
o sumo [suco] *oo soo·moo [soo·koo]*	juice
o refresco *oo reh·fray·skoo*	soda

In both Portugal and Brazil, look for the bars advertising **sumo [suco]** (juice) with lots of fresh fruit on display. **Sumol**® is the oldest brand name of fruit juice and is found in almost every shop selling food. It is a lightly carbonated orange drink.

YOU MAY HEAR...

Posso oferecer-lhe uma bebida? *paw·soo aw·freh·sehr·lyeh oo·muh beh·bee·thuh*	Can I get you a drink?
Com leite/açúcar? *kaumlayt/uh·soo·kuhr*	With milk/sugar?
Água com ou sem gás? *ah·gwuh kaum auoo seng gahz*	Carbonated or non-carbonated [still] water?

Aperitifs, Cocktails & Liqueurs

aguardente de... *ah·gwahr·thent deh...*	tequila with...
figo *fee·goo*	fig
medronho *meh·draw·nyoo*	arbutus berry (a small strawberry-like fruit)
velha *veh·lyuh*	brandy
a batida... *uh buh·tee·duh...*	cane spirit with fruit juice, sugar, ice and...(Braz.)

de cajú *deh kuh·zsoo*	cashew nut
de coco *deh kau·koo*	coconut
de maracujá *deh muh·ruh·koo·zsah*	passion fruit
a caipirinha *uh keye·pee·ree·nyuh*	cane spirit, crushed lime, sugar and ice (Braz.)
a Cuba livre *uh koo·buh lee·vreh*	rum and Coke®
a genebra *uh zseh·neh·bruh*	gin
a ginjinha *uh zseeng·zsee·nyuh*	spirit distilled from morello cherries
o uísque *oo wees·keh*	whiskey
o vermute *oo vehr·moot*	vermouth
a tequila *uh teh·kee·luh*	tequila
o rum *oo roong*	rum
a vodca *uh vaw·dee·kuh*	vodka

Beer

a cerveja *uh sehr·vay·zsuh*	beer
a cerveja branca *uh sehr·vay·zsuh bruhn·kuh*	lager
a cerveja preta *uh sehr·vay·zsuh preh·tuh*	dark beer
cerveja leve *sehr·veh·zsuh leh·veh*	light beer
a imperial [um chope] *uh eem·peh·ree·ahl [oo shaw·pee]*	draft [draught] beer
engarrafada *ehn·guh·ruh·fah·duh*	bottled
local/importada *loo·kahl/eem·pawr·tah·duh*	local imported
sem álcool *seng ahl·kawl*	non-alcoholic

Beer is a popular drink in Portugal and Brazil. Try local brews, such as **Sagres** or **Super Bock** in Portugal and **Antártica** in Brazil. In Portugal, beer is often served with **tremoços** (salted lupini beans) or **amendoins** (peanuts).

Wine

o vinho... *oo vee·nyoo...*   ...wine

   de casa/mesa *deh kah·zuh/meh·zuh*   house/table

   (da) Madeira *(thuh) muh·thay·ruh*   (from) Madeira

   (do) Porto *(thoo) paur·too*   Port

   espumante *ee·spoo·muhnt*   sparkling

   seco/doce *seh·koo/dau·seh*   dry/sweet

   tinto/branco/rosé *teen·too/bruhn·koo/raw·zeh*   red/white/blush [rosé]

   verde *vehrd*   dry white wine

Brazilian wines are produced in the southern part of the country, which turns out some good reds and whites. Labels to look for include **Almadén** and **Forestier**.

Excellent red and white aperitif and dessert wines come from the island of Madeira; **Sercial** is the driest, and **Verdelho** (medium-dry) can be drunk as an aperitif; **Boal** (or **Bual**) is smoky and less sweet than the rich dark-amber **Malvásia** (or Malsey), which is best served as a dessert wine at room temperature.

Port, famous fortified wine from the upper Douro valley, east of Oporto, is classified by vintage and blend. The vintage ports, only made in exceptional years, are harvested and left to ferment for at least two years before being bottled, and then stored for ten to twenty years. The blended ports are kept in barrels for a minimum of five years. There are two types: the younger ruby variety (**tinto aloirado**) is full-colored and full-bodied, while the tawny (**aloirado**) is less sweet, amber-colored and delicate.

Vinho verde, green wine, produced in northwest Portugal, is made from unripened grapes. It is faintly sparkling and acidic in taste, with a low alcohol content.

On the Menu

o abacate *oo uh•buh•kaht*   avocado
o abacaxi *oo uh•buh•kah•shee*   pineapple
a abóbora *uh uh•baw•boo•ruh*   pumpkin
o açafrão *oo uh•suh•frohm*   saffron
o acarajé *oo uh•kuh•ruh•zseh*   fried beans
o açúcar *oo uh•soo•kuhr*   sugar
o agrião *oo uh•gree•ohm*   watercress
a água *uh ah•gwuh*   water
a água de coco *uh ah•gwuh deh kau•koo*   coconut juice
a água mineral *uh ah•gwuh mee•neh•ral*   mineral water
o aipo *oo ah•ee•poo*   celery
a alcachofra *uh ahl•kuh•shau•fruh*   artichoke
as alcaparras *uhz ahl•kuh•pah•rruhz*   capers
o alecrim *oo uh•leh•kreeng*   rosemary
a aletria *uh uhl•eh•tree•uh*   sweet noodle pudding
a alface *uh ahl•fah•seh*   lettuce
à Algarvia *ah uhl•guhr•vee•uh*   almond layer cake
a alheira *uh ah•lyay•ruh*   sausage
o alho *oo ah•lyoo*   garlic

o alho porro _oo ah·lyoo pau·rroo_	leek
o almoço _oo ahl·mau·soo_	lunch
as almôndegas _uhz ahl·mawn·deh·guhz_	fishballs or meatballs
o alperce _oo uhl·pehr·seh_	apricot
as amêijoas _uhz uh·may·zsoo·uhz_	baby clams
as ameixas _uhz uh·may·shuhz_	plums
as ameixas secas _uhz uh·may·shuhz seh·kuhz_	prunes
a amêndoa _uh uh·mehn·doo·uh_	almond
o amendoim _oo uh·mehn·doo·eeng_	peanut
a amora _uh uh·maw·ruh_	blackberry
o ananás _oo uh·nuh·nahz_	pineapple
a anchova _uh uhn·shau·vuh_	anchovy
o aperitivo _oo uh·pehr·uh·tee·voo_	aperitif
o arenque _oo uh·rehn·keh_	herring
o arroz _oo uh·rrauz_	rice
o arroz doce _oo uh·rrauz dau·seh_	rice pudding
o assado _oo uh·sah·thoo_	roast
o atum _oo uh·toong_	tuna
a aveia _uh uh·vay·uh_	oats
a avelã _uh uh·veh·luh_	hazelnut
as aves _uhz ahv·ehz_	poultry
a azeda _uh uh·zeh·duh_	sorrel
azedo _uh·zeh·thoo_	sour
o azeite _oo uh·zay·teh_	oil
az azeitonas _uhz uh·zay·tau·nuhz_	olive
o bacalhau _oo buh·kuh·lyahoo_	cod
a banana _uh buh·nuh·nuh_	banana
a batata _uh buh·tah·tuh_	potato
a batata doce _uh buh·tah·tuh dau·seh_	sweet potato
as batatas fritas _uhz buh·tah·tuhz free·tuhz_	fries [chips]
o batido _oo buh·tee·thoo_	milk shake

a baunilha *uh bahoo-nee-lyuh*	vanilla
a bebida *uh beh-bee-thuh*	drink
o berbigão *oo behr-bee-gohm*	type of cockle
a beringela *uh behr-eeng-zseh-luh*	eggplant [aubergine]
o besugo *oo beh-soo-goo*	bream(fish)
a beterraba *uh beh-teh-rrah-buh*	beet [beetroot]
o bife *oo beef*	steak
o bife acebolado *oo beef uh-seh-boo-lah-thoo*	steak with onions (Braz.)
a bola de Berlim *uh bau-luh deh behr-leeng*	doughnut
a bolacha *uh boo-lah-shuh*	cookie [biscuit]
a bolacha de água e sal *uh boo-lah-shuh deh ah-gwuh ee sahl*	cracker
o bolo *oo bau-loo*	pastry
o borrego *oo boo-rreh-goo*	lamb
as broas castelares *uhz brau-uhz kuhz-tuh-lay-rehz*	sweet-potato cookies
as broas de mel *uhz brau-uhz deh mehl*	corn flour and honey cookies
os brócolos *ooz braw-koo-looz*	broccoli
os bunuelos *ooz boo-noo-eh-looz*	dough fritters (Braz.)
o cabrito *oo kuh-bree-too*	kid
a caça *uh kah-suh*	game
o cacau *oo kuh-kahoo*	cocoa
o cachorro quente *oo kuh-shau-roo kehnt*	hot dog
o café *oo kuh-feh*	coffee
o caju *oo kah-zsoo*	cashew nut (Braz.)
a caldeirada *uh kahl-day-rah-duh*	fish stew
o caldo *oo kahl-doo*	consommé
o caldo de cana *oo kahl-doo deh kuh-nuh*	sugar-cane juice
o caldo verde *oo kahl-doo vehrd*	potato and kale soup
os camarões *ooz kuh-muh-roings*	shrimp
o canapé *oo kuh-nuh-peh*	small open sandwich

a canela *uh kuh·neh·luh* — cinnamon

a canja *uh keng·juh* — chicken soup with rice

o capão *oo cuh·pohm* — capon

o caqui *oo kuh·kee* — persimmon (Braz.)

o caracol *oo kuh·ruh·kawl* — snail; spiral bun with currant█

o caranguejo *oo kuh·ruhn·gay·zsoo* — crab

o carapau *oo kuh·ruh·pahoo* — mackerel

o caril *oo kuh·reel* — curry powder

a carne de porco *uh kahr·neh deh paur·koo* — pork

a carne de sol *uh kahr·neh deh sawl* — sun-dried meat, jerky

a carne de vaca *uh kahr·neh deh vah·kuh* — beef

a carne picada *uh kahr·neh pee·kah·thuh* — minced meat

o carneiro *oo kuhrr·nay·roo* — mutton

as carnes *uhz kahr·nehz* — meat

as carnes frias *uhz kahr·nehz free·uhz* — [charcuterie] cold cuts

o caruru *oo kuh·roo·roo* — minced herbs in oil and spices (Braz.)

caseiro *oo kuh·zay·roo* — homemade

a casquinha de siri *uh kuhz·kee·nyuh deh see·ree* — crab in its shell (Braz.)

a castanha *uh kuhz·tuh·nyuh* — chestnut

a castanha de caju *uh kuhz·tuh·nyuh deh kah·zsoo* — cashew nut

a (água de) Castelo *uh (ah·gwuh deh) kuh·steh·loo* — carbonated mineral water

a cavala *uh kuh·vuh·luh* — mackerel

a cebola *uh seh·bau·luh* — onion

a cenoura *uh seh·nau·ruh* — carrot

a cereja *uh seh·ray·zsuh* — cherry

o chá *oo shah* — tea

o chá com leite *oo shah kaum layt* — tea with milk

o chá com limão *oo shah kaumlee·mohm*	tea with lemon
o chá de limão *oo shah deh lee·mohm*	tea made fromlemon peel infusion
o chá maté *oo shah muh·teh*	tea infused with maté-tree leaf
o cherne *oo shehr·neh*	black grouper
a chicória *uh shee·kaw·ree·uh*	chicory
o chispe *oo sheez·peh*	pig's foot [trotter]
o chocolate quente *oo shoo·koo·laht kehnt*	hot chocolate
os chocos *ooz shau·kooz*	cuttlefish
o chouriço *oo shaw·ree·soo*	smoked pork sausage
o chuchu *oo shoo·shoo*	type of rutabaga (Braz.)
o churrasco *oo shoo·rahz·koo*	charcoal-grilled meat
as cocadas *uhz caw·cah·duhz*	coconut macaroons (Braz.)
o coco *oo kau·koo*	coconut
a codorna *uh koo·dawrr·nuh*	quail (Braz.)
a codorniz *uh koo·dawrr·neez*	quail
o coelho *oo koo·eh·lyoo*	rabbit
o coentro *oo koo·ehn·troo*	coriander
o cogumelo *oo koo·goo·meh·loo*	button mushroom
o colorau *oo koo·loo·rahoo*	paprika
os cominhos *ooz koo·mee·nyooz*	cumin
a compota *uh koom·paw·tuh*	compote, stewed fruit
os condimentos *ooz kaum·dee·mehn·tooz*	seasonings
o congro *oo kaum·groo*	conger eel
o conhaque *oo kaw·nyahk*	cognac
a conta *uh kaum·tuh*	bill
o copo *oo kaw·poo*	glass
o coração *oo koo·ruh·sohm*	heart
o cordeiro *oo koor·day·roo*	lamb
a corvina *uh kawr·vee·nuh*	croaker (fish)

a costeleta *uh koo·stuh·leh·tuh*	cutlet
a couve *uh kaw·veh*	cabbage
a couve Portuguesa *uh kaw·veh poor·too·geh·zuh*	kale
a couve roxa *uh kaw·veh rau·shuh*	red cabbage
a couve-de-bruxelas *uh kaw·veh de broo·sheh·luhz*	brussels sprouts
a couve-flor *uh kaw·veh flaur*	cauliflower
a coxinha de galinha *uh kaw·shee·nyuh deh guh·lee·nyuh*	pastry filled with chicken
os cravinhos *ooz kruh·vee·nyooz*	cloves
o creme *oo krehm*	cream
o creme de abacate *oo krehmdeh uh·buh·kaht*	avocado with lime juice and sugar (Braz.)
o creme leite *oo krehm layt*	custard
o crepe *oo krehp*	pancake
a criação *uh kree·uh·sohm*	poultry
cru *kroo*	raw
os crustáceos *ooz kroo·stah·see·ooz*	shellfish
o damasco *oo duh·mahs·koo*	apricot (Braz.)
a dendê *uh dehn·deh*	palmoil
o doce de abóbora *oo thaus deh uh·baw·boo·ruh*	pumpkin dessert
o doce de fruta [a geleia] *oo thaus deh froo·tuh [uh zseh·lay·uh]*	jam
o doce de laranja *oo thaus de luh·ruhn·zsuh*	marmalade
o doce de ovos e amêndoa *oo thaus deh aw·vooz ee uh·mehn·doo·uh*	marzipan
o eiró *oo ay·raw*	eel
a empadinha *uh eem·puh·thee·nyuh*	filled pastry

o empadão de batata *oo eem·puh·dohm deh buh·tah·tuh*	shepherd's pie	
a enguia *uh eng·gee·uh*	eel	
o ensopado de cabrito *oo eng·soo·pah·thoo deh keh·bree·too*	kid stew	
a entrada *uh ehn·trah·thuh*	appetizer [starter]	
o entrecosto *oo ehn·treh·kaus·too*	sparerib	
a erva-doce *uh ehr·vuh thaus*	aniseed	
as ervilhas *uhz eer·vee·lyuhz*	peas	
escalfado *ee·skahl·fah·thoo*	poached	
o espadarte *oo ee·spah·dahr·teh*	swordfish	
os espargos *ooz ees·pahr·gooz*	asparagus	
o esparguete *oo ee·sparh·geht*	spaghetti	
os espinafres *ooz ee·spee·nah·frehz*	spinach	
estufado *ee·stoo·fah·thoo*	braised	
o esturjão *oo ee·stoor·zsohm*	sturgeon	
o faisão *oo feye·zohm*	pheasant	
a farinha *uh fuh·ree·nyuh*	flour	
a farofa *uh fuh·rau·fuh*	cassava flour	
as favas *uhz fah·vuhz*	broad beans	
o feijão *oo fay·zsohm*	bean	
o feijão branco *oo fay·zsohm bruhn·koo*	navy bean	
o feijão catarino *oo fay·zsohm kuh·tuh·ree·noo*	pink bean	
o feijão encarnado *oo fay·zsohm eng·kuhrr·nah·thoo*	red bean	
o feijão frade *oo fay·zsohm frahd*	black-eyed bean	
o feijão guisado [ensopado] *oo fay·zsohm gee·sah·thoo [een·soo·pah·doo]*	beans with bacon in tomato sauce	
o feijão preto *oo fay·zsohm preh·too*	black bean	
o feijão tropeiro *oo fay·zsohm trau·pay·roo*	black beans fried with jerky (Braz.)	

o feijão verde _oo fay·zsohm vehrd_	green beans
o fiambre _oo fee·uhm·breh_	boiled ham
o fígado _oo fee·guh·doo_	liver
o figo _oo fee·goo_	fig
o filé _oo fee·leh_	steak (Braz.)
o filete _oo fee·leht_	fillet of fish
o folhado _oo foo·lyah·thoo_	sweet puff-pastry
as filhós _uhz fee·lyawz_	fritters
a framboesa _uh fruhm·boo·eh·zuh_	raspberry
o frango _oo fruhn·goo_	chicken
o frango assado _oo fruhn·goo uh·sah·thoo_	roast chicken
a fritada de peixe _uh free·tah·duh deh paysh_	deep-fried fish
a fruta _uh froo·tuh_	fruit
a fruta do conde _uh froo·tuh thoo kaum·deh_	custard apple
a fruta em calda _uh froo·tuh eng kahl·duh_	fruit in syrup
os frutos do mar _ooz froo·tuhz thoo mahr_	seafood
a fubá _uh foo·bah_	corn flour (Braz.)
a galantina _uh guh·luhn·tee·nuh_	pressed meat in gelatin
o galão _oo guh·lohm_	weak milky coffee
a galinha _uh guh·lee·nyuh_	stewing chicken
a galinhola _uh guh·lee·nyaw·luh_	woodcock
as gambas _uhz guhm·buhz_	shrimp [king prawns]
o ganso _oo guhn·soo_	goose
a garoupa _uh guh·rauoo·puh_	large grouper (fish)
a garrafa _uh guh·rrah·fuh_	bottle
a gasosa _uh guh·zaw·zuh_	lemonade
o gaspacho _oo guhz·pah·shoo_	chilled soup
o gelado _oo zseh·lah·thoo_	ice cream
a gelatina _uh zseh·luh·tee·nuh_	jelly
a geleia _uh zseh·lay·uh_	jelly (Braz.)
o gelo _oo zseh·loo_	ice

o gengibre *oo zsehn-zsee-breh* — ginger

a goiaba *uh zsoy-ah-buh* — guava (Braz.)

a goiabada *uh zsoy-uh-bah-duh* — thick paste made of guava (Braz.)

o gombo *oo gaum-boo* — okra (Braz.)

os grelos *ooz greh-looz* — turnip sprouts

a groselha *uh groo-zeh-lyuh* — red currant

o guisado *oo gee-zah-thoo* — stew

a hortaliça *uh awr-tuh-lee-suh* — fresh vegetables

a hortelã *uh awr-teh-luh* — mint

o inhame *oo ee-nuhm* — yam

oo iogurte *oo yaw-goort* — yogurt

a isca de peixe *uh ees-kuh deh paysh* — fried small fish (Braz.)

as iscas *uhz ees-kuhz* — sliced liver

a jabuticaba *uh juh-boo-tee-cah-buh* — type of cherry (Braz.)

a jardineira *uh zsuhr-dee-nay-ruh* — mixed vegetables

o javali *oo zsuh-vah-li* — wild boar

o kibe *oo keeb* — meat and bulgur croquette (Braz.)

o kiwi *oo kee-vee* — kiwi

a lagosta *uh lah-gau-stuh* — lobster

o lagostim *oo luh-gau-steeng* — crayfish

lagostim do-rio *luh-gau-steeng doo ree-oo* — fresh-water crayfish

a lampreia *uh luhm-pray-uh* — lamprey

a laranja *uh luh-ruhn-zsuh* — orange

a laranjada *uh luh-ruhn-zsah-thuh* — orange soda

o lavagante *oo luh-vu-guhnt* — lobster

a lebre *uh leh-breh* — hare

os legumes *ooz leh-goomz* — vegetables

o leite *oo layt* — milk

o leite de coco *oo layt deh kau-koo* — coconut milk

o leitão *oo lay•tohm*	suckling pig
as lentilhas *uhz lehn•tee•lyuhz*	lentils
a lima *uh lee•muh*	lime
o limão *oo lee•mohm*	lemon
o limão verde *oo lee•mohm vehrd*	lime (Braz.)
a língua *uh leen•gwuh*	tongue
o linguado *oo leen•gwah•doo*	sole
a linguiça *uh leen•gwee•suh*	thin sausage
o lombo *oo laum•boo*	loin
o louro *oo lau•roo*	bay leaf
a lula *uh loo•luh*	squid
a maçã *uh muh•suh*	apple
o maçapão *oo muh•suh•pohm*	marzipan
o macarrão *oo muh•kuh•rrohm*	macaroni
a macaxeira *uh muh•kuh•shay•ruh*	cassava root (Braz.)
maduro *muh•thoo•roo*	ripe
a maionese *uh meye•aw•nehz*	mayonnaise
a malagueta *uh muh•luh•geh•tuh*	hot pepper
as malsadas *uhz mahl•sah•duhz*	fried dough (Braz.)
o mamão *oo muh•mohm*	papaya
a mandioca *uh muhn•dee•aw•kuh*	cassava root (Braz.)
a manga *uh muhn•guh*	mango
o manjericão *oo muhn•zsehr•ee•kohm*	basil
a manteiga *uh muhn•tay•guh*	butter
o maracujá *oo muh•ruh•koo•zsah*	passion fruit (Braz.)
os mariscos *ooz muh•rees•kooz*	seafood
a marmelada *uh muhr•meh•lah•duh*	thick quince paste
a massa *uh mah•suh*	pasta; dough; pastry
o massapão *oo muh•suh•pohm*	marzipan
os massapães *ooz muh•suh•pengz*	almond macaroons
o mate *oo maht*	tea with maté leaf (Braz.)

o medalhão *oo meh·deh·lyohm* — tenderloin steak

o medronho *oo meh·drau·nyoo* — arbutus berry (small strawberry-like fruit)

o mel *oo mehl* — honey

a melancia *uh muh·luhn·see·uh* — watermelon

o melão *oo meh·lohm* — melon

o melão com presunto *oo meh·lohm kaumpreh·zoon·too* — melon with ham

o mero *oo meh·roo* — red grouper (fish)

a mexerica *uh meh·sheh·ree·kuh* — tangerine (Braz.)

os mexilhões *ooz meh·shee·lyoings* — mussels

as migas de bacalhau *uhz mee·guhz deh buh·kuh·lyahoo* — dried cod soup

o milho *oo mee·lyoo* — sweet corn

os miolos *ooz mee·aw·looz* — brains

o misto quente *oo mee·stoo kehnt* — ham-and-cheese toasted sandwich (Braz.)

o morango *oo moo·ruhn·goo* — strawberry

a morcela *uh moor·seh·luh* — blood sausage [black pudding]

a mortadela *uh moor·tuh·deh·luh* — mortadella

a mostarda *uh moo·stahr·duh* — mustard

a mousse de chocolate *uh moo·seh deh shoo·koo·laht* — chocolate pudding

a mousse de maracujá *uh moo·seh deh muh·ruh·koo·zsah* — passion fruit mousse

as nabiças *uhz nuh·bee·suhz* — turnip greens

os nabos *ooz nah·booz* — turnips

a nata *uh nah·tuh* — fresh cream

a nata batida *uh nah·tuh buh·tee·duh* — whipped cream

(ao) natural *(ahoo) nuh·too·rahl* — plain

as nêsperas uhz neh·speh·ruhz	loquat (fruit)
no forno noo faurr·noo	baked
a noz uh nawz	nut
a noz moscada uh nawz moo·skah·thuh	nutmeg
o óleo oo aw·lee·oo	oil
o óleo de amendoim oo aw·lee·oo deh uh·mehn·doo·eeng	peanut oil
a omelete uh aw·meh·leht	omelet
o orégão [orégano] oo aw·reh·gohm	oregano
o osso oo au·soo	bone
a ostra uh aw·struh	oyster
o ovo oo aw·voo	egg
os ovos cozidos ooz aw·vooz koo·zee·thooz	boiled eggs
os ovos escalfados ooz aw·vooz ees·kahl·fah·thooz	poached eggs
os ovos estrelados [fritos] ooz aw·vooz ees·truh·lah·dooz [free·tooz]	fried eggs
os ovos mexidos ooz aw·vooz meh·shee·dooz	scrambled eggs
os ovos quentes ooz aw·vooz kehntz	soft-boiled eggs
o palmito oo pahl·mee·too	palmhearts (Braz.)
panado [empanado] puh·nah·thoo [ehm·puh·nah·doo]	breaded
a panqueca uh puhn·keh·kuh	pancake
o pão (escuro/integral) oo pohm (ees·koo·roo/een·teh·grahl)	bread (brown/whole wheat)
o pão de centeio oo pohmdeh sehn·tay·oo	rye bread
o pão-de-ló oo pohm·deh·law	coffee cake
o pãozinho oo pohm·zee·nyoo	bread roll
o pargo oo pahr·goo	bream(fish)
as passas (de uva) uhz pah·suhz (deh oo·vuh)	raisin

assado *puh·sah·thoo*	cooked (meat, etc.)
pastel *oo puhs·tehl*	small pie
pato *oo pah·too*	duck
pé de moleque *oo peh deh maw·leh·keh*	peanut brittle (Braz.)
peito de galinha *oo pay·too deh uh·lee·nyuh*	chicken breast
peixe *oo paysh*	fish
peixe-agulha *oo paysh·uh·goo·lya*	garfish
peixe-espada *oo paysh ees·pah·duh*	swordfish
pepino *oo peh·pee·noo*	cucumber
pepino de conserva *oo peh·pee·noo deh kaum·sehr·vuh*	pickle [gherkin]
a **pêra** *uh peh·ruh*	pear
a **perca** *uh pehr·kuh*	perch
a **perdiz** *uh pehr·deez*	partridge
a **perna de galinha** *uh pehrr·nuh deh guh·lee·nyuh*	chicken leg
o **pernil** *oo perr·neel*	ham
o **pêro** *oo peh·rau*	variety of apple
o **peru** *oo peh·roo*	turkey
os **pés de porco** *ooz pehz deh paur·koo*	pig's feet [trotters]
a **pescada** *uh pehz·kah·thuh*	whiting
o **pêssego** *oo peh·suh·goo*	peach
os **petiscos** *ooz peh·tees·kooz*	appetizers [starters]
a **pevide** *uh peh·veed*	salted pumpkin seed
a **picanha desfiada** *uh pee·kuh·nyuh dehs·fee·ah·thuh*	charcoal-grilled meat (Braz.)
os **pickles** *ooz pee·kehlz*	pickled vegetables
a **pimenta** *uh pee·mehn·tuh*	pepper
os **pimentos assados** *ooz pee·mehn·tooz uh·sah·dooz*	roasted peppers

o pinhão *oo pee·nyohm*	nut
a pinhoada *uh pee·nyoo·ah·duh*	pine nut brittle
o pipis *oo pee·peez*	spicy giblet stew
o pirarucu *oo pee·ruh·roo·koo*	type of fish (Braz.)
o piri-piri *oo pee·ree pee·ree*	seasoning of hot chili pepp and olive oil
o polvo *oo paul·voo*	octopus
o pombo *oo paum·boo*	pigeon
o porco *oo paur·koo*	pork
a posta *uh paws·tuh*	slice of fish or meat
o presunto *oo preh·zoon·too*	cured ham
o presunto cru *oo preh·zoon·too kroo*	dried ham
o pudim flan *oo poo·deeng fluhn*	caramel custard
o puré de batatas *oo poo·reh deh buh·tah·tuhz*	mashed potatoes
a queijada *uh kay·zsah·duh*	small cottage-cheese tart
o queijinho do céu *oo kay·zsee·nyoo doo sehoo*	marzipan balls rolled in sug
o queijo *oo kay·zsoo*	cheese
o quiabo *oo kee·ah·boo*	okra
o quindim *oo keeng·deeng*	pudding made with coconu and egg yolks (Braz.)

a rabanada *uh ruh·buh·nah·duh*	French toast
o rabanete *oo ruh·buh·neht*	radish
a raia *uh reye·uh*	skate (fish)
a rainha-cláudia *uh ray·ee·nyuh klaw·dee·uh*	greengage plum
recheado *reh·shee·ah·thoo*	stuffed
o recheio *oo re·shay·oo*	stuffing
o refogado *oo reh·foo·gah·thoo*	onions fried in olive oil
o refresco *oo reh·frehs·koo*	soft drink
o repolho *oo rreh·pau·lyoo*	cabbage
o requeijão *oo rre·kay·zsohm*	curd cheese (Braz.)
o rim *oo rreeng*	kidney
o robalo *oo rraw·buh·loo*	sea bass
o rodízio *oo rroo·dee·zee·oo*	selection of chargrilled meats (Braz.)
a romã *uh rrau·muh*	pomegranate
a rosca *uh rraus·kuh*	ring-shaped white bread
o rosmaninho *oo rrooz·muh·neeng·nyoo*	rosemary
o ruivo *oo rroo·ee·voo*	red gurnard (fish)
o sal *oo sahl*	salt
a salada *uh suh·lah·duh*	salad
a salada de alface/escarola *uh suh·lah·duh deh ahl·fah·seh/ees·kuh·raw·luh*	green salad
a salada de agrião *uh suh·lah·duh deh uh·gree·ohm*	watercress salad
a salada mista *uh suh·lah·duh mees·tuh*	tomato and lettuce salad
salgado *sahl·gah·thoo*	salted
o salmão (fumado) [defumado] *oo suh·mohm (foo·mah·thoo) [deh·foo·mah·do]*	(smoked) salmon
o salmonete *oo sahl·moo·neht*	red mullet
a salsa *uh sahl·suh*	parsley
a salsicha *uh sahl·see·shuh*	sausage

salteado sahl·tee·ah·thoo	sautéed
a salva uh sahl·vuh	sage
as sandes uhz suhndz	sandwich
a sanduíche uh suhn·doo·eesh	sandwich
a santola uh suhn·taw·luh	spider-crab
o sarapatel oo suh·ruh·puh·tehl	pork or mutton stew
a sarda uh sahr·thuh	mackerel
as sardinhas uhz suhr·dee·nyuhz	sardines
o sável oo sah·vehl	shad (herring-like fish)
seco seh·koo	dry
a sêmola uh seh·moo·luh	semolina
o sericá alentejano oo seh·ree·kah uh·lehn·teh·zsuh·noo	cinnamon soufflé
a sidra uh see·druh	cider
o siri oo see·ree	crab (Braz.)
as sobremesas uhz sau·breh·meh·zuhz	dessert
a solha uh sau·lyuh	plaice (fish)
o sonho oo sau·nyoo	type of doughnut
a sopa uh sau·puh	soup
o sorvete oo sawr·veht	ice cream (Braz.)
o sumo [suco] oo soo·moo [soo·koo]	fruit juice
o sururu oo soo·roo·roo	type of cockle (Braz.)
o suspiro oo soo·spee·roo	meringue
a taínha uh tah·ee·nyuh	gray mullet (fish)
a tâmara uh tuh·muh·ruh	date
a tangerina uh tuhn·zsuh·ree·nuh	tangerine
a tarte de amêndoa uh tahrt de uh·mehn·doo·uh	almond tart
o tempero oo tehm·peh·roo	seasoning
tenro tehn·rroo	tender
o tomate oo too·maht	tomato

o tomilho *oo too-mee-lyoo* — thyme

a toranja *uh tau-ruhn-zsuh* — grapefruit

as torradas *uhz too-rrah-duhz* — toast

o torrão de ovos *oo too-rrohm deh aw-vooz* — marzipan candy

a tosta *uh taw-stuh* — toasted sandwich

o toucinho *oo tau-see-nyoo* — bacon

o tremoço *oo treh-maw-soo* — salted lupin bean

a trufa *uh troo-fuh* — truffle

a truta *uh troo-tuh* — trout

o tucupi *oo too-koo-pee* — cassava juice (Braz.)

o tutano *oo too-tuh-noo* — marrow

o umbu *oo oom-boo* — tropical fruit (Braz.)

as uvas *uhz oo-vuhz* — grapes

as vagens *uhz vah-gehnz* — green beans

variado *vuh-ree-ah-thoo* — assorted

o veado *oo vee-ah-thoo* — venison

os vegetais variados *ooz veh-zseh-teyez vuh-ree-ah-thooz* — mixed vegetables

a vieira *uh vee-ay-ruh* — scallop

o vinagre *oo vee-nah-greh* — vinegar

a vitela *uh vee-tehl-uh* — veal

People

ESSENTIAL

Hello.	**Olá.** _aw·lah_
How are you?	**Como está?** _kau·moo ee·stah_
Fine, thanks.	**Bem, obrigado _m_ /obrigada _f_.** _behm_ _aw·bree·gah·doo/aw·bree·gah·duh_
Excuse me! (to get attention)	**Desculpe!** _dehz·kool·peh_
Do you speak English?	**Fala inglês?** _fah·luh eeng·lehz_
What's your name?	**Como se chama?** _kau·moo seh shuh·muh_
My name is...	**Chamo-me... [Meu nome é...]** _shuh·moo meh... [mehoo naum·ee eh...]_
Nice to meet you.	**Muito prazer.** _mooee·too pruh·zehr_
Where are you from?	**De onde é?** _deh aund eh_
I'm from the U.S./U.K.	**Sou dos Estados Unidos/da Inglaterra.** _soh dooz ee·stah·dooz oo·nee·dooz/duh eeng·luh·teh·rruh_
What do you do?	**O que é que faz?** _oo kee eh keh fahz_
I work for...	**Trabalho para...** _truh·bah·lyoo puh·ruh..._
I'm a student.	**Sou estudante.** _sauoo ee·stoo·duhnt_
I'm retired.	**Sou reformado _m_ /reformada _f_ [aposentado _m_ /aposentada _f_].** _soh reh·foor·mah·thoo/ reh·foor·mah·thuh [uh·poo·zehn·tah·doo/ uh·poo·zehn·tah·duh]_
Do you like...?	**Gosta de...?** _gaw·stuh deh..._
Goodbye.	**Adeus.** _uh·deeooz_
See you later.	**Até mais tarde.** _uh·teh meyez tahrd_

In Portuguese, there are a number of forms for 'you' (taking different verb forms): **tu** (singular) and **vós** (plural) are used when talking to relatives, close friends and children; **você** (singular) and **vocês** (plural) are used in all other cases. If in doubt, use **você/ vocês**.

Language Difficulties

Do you speak English?	**Fala inglês?** _fah·luh eeng·lehz_
Does anyone here speak English?	**Há aqui alguém que fale inglês?** _ah uh·kee ahl·gehng keh fah·leh eeng·lehz_
I don't speak (much) Portuguese.	**Não falo (muito) português.** _nohm fah·loo (mooee·too) poor·too·gehz_
Could you speak more slowly?	**Pode falar mais devagar?** _pawd fuh·lahr meyez deh·vuh·gahr_
Could you repeat that?	**Pode repetir?** _pawd reh·peh·teer_
Excuse me? [Pardon?]	**Faça favor?** _fah·suh fuh·vaur_
What was that?	**Como disse?** _kau·moo dee·seh_
Could you spell it?	**Pode soletrar?** _pawd sau·leh·trahr_
Please write it down.	**Escreva, por favor.** _ee·screhv poor fuh·vaur_
Can you translate this for me?	**Pode traduzir-me isto?** _pawd truh·doo·zeer·meh ee·stoo_
What does this/that mean?	**O que significa isto/aquilo?** _oo keh sehg·nee·fee·kuh ee·stoo/uh·kee·loo_
I understand.	**Compreendo [Entendo].** _kaum·pree·ehn·doo [ehn·tehn·doo]_
I don't understand.	**Não compreendo [entendo].** _nohm kaum·pree·ehn·doo [ehn·tehn·doo]_
Do you understand?	**Entende?** _ehn·tehn·deh_

YOU MAY HEAR...

Falo só um pouco de Inglês. _fah_•loo saw
oong _pau_•koo deh eeng•_lehz_

I only speak a little
English.

Nao falo Inglês. nohm _fah_•loo eeng•_lehz_

I don't speak English.

Making Friends

Hello.	**Olá.** aw•_lah_
Good morning.	**Bom dia.** bong _dee_•uh
Good afternoon.	**Boa tarde.** _baw_•uh tahrd
Good evening.	**Boa noite.** _baw_•uh noyt
My name is...	**Chamo-me... [Meu nome é...]** _shuh_•moo meh... [mehoo _naum_•ee eh...]
What's your name?	**Como se chama?** _kau_•moo seh _shuh_•muh
I'd like to introduce you to...	**Gostaria de te apresentar ao/à...** goo•stuh•_ree_•uh deh the uh•preh•sehn•_tahr_ ahoo/ah...
Nice to meet you.	**Muito prazer.** _mooee_•too preh•_zehr_
How are you?	**Como está?** _kau_•moo ee•_stah_

Fine, thanks.	**Bem, obrigado** *m* **/obrigada** *f.* *beng*
	aw•bree•gah•doo/aw•bree•gah•duh
And you?	**E o senhor** *m* **/a senhora** *f*? *ee oo seh•nyaur/uh*
	seh•nyau•ruh

In both Portugal and Brazil, a standard greeting is a handshake accompanied by direct eye contact and the appropriate greeting for the time of day. Once a closer relationship has developed, greetings become more personal: men may greet each other with a hug, and women kiss each other twice on the cheek starting with the right. Anyone with a university degree is referred to as **Senhor Doutor** (literally, Mr. Doctor) if male or **Senhora Doutora** (Ms. Doctor) if female. Wait until invited before moving to a first-name basis.

Travel Talk

I'm here...	**Estou aqui...** *ee•stawoo uh•kee...*
on business	**em negócios** *eng neh•gaw•see•yooz*
on vacation [holiday]	**de férias** *deh feh•ree•uhz*
studying	**a estudar [estudando]** *uh ee•stoo•dahr*
	[ee•stoo•duhn•doo]
I'm staying for...	**Fico por...** *fee•koo poor...*
I've been here...	**Eu já estive aqui...** *ehoo zsah ee•stee•veh uh•kee...*
a day	**um dia** *oong dee•uh*
a week	**uma semana** *oo•muh seh•muh•nuh*
a month	**um mês** *oong mehz*
Where are you from?	**De onde é?** *deh aund eh*
I'm from...	**Sou...** *sawoo...*

For Numbers, see page 173.

Personal

Who are you with?	**Com quem está?**	kaun keng ee·*stah*
I'm on my own.	**Estou sozinho** m /**sozinha** f.	ee·*stawoo* saw·*zee*·nyoo/saw·*zee*·nyuh
I'm with my...	**Estou com o meu** m /**a minha** f...	ee·*stawoo* kaum oo mehoo/uh *mee*·nyuh...
husband/wife	**marido/mulher**	muh·*ree*·thoo/moo·*lyehr*
boyfriend/girlfriend	**namorado/namorada**	nuh·moo·*rah*·thoo/ nuh·moo·*rah*·thuh
friend(s)	**amigo(s)** m /**amiga(s)** f	uh·*mee*·goo(z)/ uh·*mee*·guh(z)
colleague(s)	**colega(s)**	koo·*leh*·guh(z)
When's your birthday?	**Quando faz anos?**	*kwuhn*·doo fahz uh·noos
How old are you?	**Quantos anos tens?**	*kwuhn*·tooz uh·noos tengz
I'm...	**Eu tenho...**	ehoo *teh*·nyoo...
Are you married?	**É casado** m /**casada** f?	eh kuh·*zah*·doo/kuh·*zah*·duh
I'm...	**Sou.../Estou...**	sawoo/ee·*stawoo*...
single	**solteiro** m /**solteira** f	saul·*tay*·roo/(saul·*tay*·ruh)
in a relationship	**num relacionamento**	noong reh·luh·see·oo·nuh·*mehn*·too
I'm...	**Sou.../Estou...**	sawoo/ee·*stawoo*...
engaged	**comprometido**	kaum·proo·meh·tee·doo
married	**casado** m /**casada** f	kuh·*zah*·doo/kuh·*zah*·duh
divorced	**divorciado** m /**divorciada** f	dee·voor·see·*ah*·doo/ dee·voor·see·*ah*·duh
separated	**separado** m /**separada** f	seh·puh·*rah*·doo/ seh·puh·*rah*·duh
I'm widowed.	**Sou viúvo** m /**viúva** f.	sau vee·*oo*·voo/vee·*oo*·vuh
Do you have children/grandchildren?	**Tem filhos/netos?**	teng *fee*·lyooz/*neh*·tooz

For Numbers, see page 173.

Work & School

What do you do?	**O que é que faz?** oo kee eh keh fahz
What are you studying?	**O que é que está a estudar [estudando]?** oo kee eh keh ee•stah uh ee•stoo•dahr [ee•stoo•duhn•doo]
I'm studying...	**Estudo...** ee•stoo•doo...
I work full time/ part time.	**Trabalho tempo integral/meio tempo.** truh•bah•lyoo tehm•poo een•teh•grahl/may•oo tehm•poo
I'm between jobs.	**Estou entre empregos.** ee•stawoo ehn•treh ehng•preh•gooz
I'm unemployed.	**Estou desempregado.** ee•stawoo deh•zehm•preh•gah•doo.
I work at home.	**Trabalho em casa.** truh•bah•lyoo eng kah•zuh
Who do you work for?	**Para quem trabalha?** puh•ruh keng truh•bah•lyuh
I work for...	**Trabalho para...** truh•bah•lyoo puh•ruh...
Here's my business card.	**Aqui está meu cartão.** uh•kee ee•stah mehoo kuhr•tohm

For Business Travel, see page 147.

Weather

What's the weather forecast?	**Quais são as previsões do tempo?** kweyez sohm uhz preh•vee•zoings thoo tehm•poo
What beautiful/ terrible weather!	**Que tempo tão lindo/ruim!** keh tehm•poo tohm leen•doo/rroo•eeng
It's cool/warm.	**Está fresco/calor.** ee•stah frehs•koo/kuh•laur
It's hot/cold.	**Está calor/frio.** ee•stah kuh•laur/free-oo.
It's rainy/sunny.	**Está um dia de chuva/sol.** ee•stah oong dee•uh deh shoo•vuh/sawl
It's snowy/icy.	**Está um dia de neve/com gelo.** ee•stah oong dee•uh deh nehv/kaum zseh•loo
Do I need a jacket/ an umbrella?	**Preciso de um casaco/guarda-chuva?** preh•see•zoo deh oong kuh•zah•koo/goo•ahr•dah shoo•vuh

Romance

ESSENTIAL

Would you like to go out for a drink/dinner?	**Queres ir tomar uma bebida/comer fóra?** *keh•rehz eer too•mahr oo•muh beh•bee•thuh/ koo•mehr faw•ruh*
What are your plans for tonight/tomorrow?	**Quais são os seus planos para hoje à noite/ amanhã?** *kweyez sohm ooz sehooz pluh•nooz puh•ruh auzseh ah noyt/uh•muh•nyuh*
Can I have your number?	**Podes dar-me o teu número de telefone?** *pawd•ehz dahr•meh oo tehoo noo•meh•roo deh tehl•fawn*
Can I join you?	**Posso acompanhar-te?** *paw•soo uh•kaum•puh•nyahr•teh*
Can I buy you a drink?	**O que quer beber?** *oo keh kehr beh•behr*
I like you.	**Gosto de ti.** *gawzh•too deh tee*
I love you.	**Amo-te [Te amo].** *uh•moo teh [teh uh•moo]*

The Dating Game

Would you like to go out for…?	**Queres ir sair para…?** *kehrz eer seh•eer puh•ruh…*
coffee	**um café** *oong kuh•feh*
a drink	**uma bebida** *oo•muh beh•bee•thuh*
dinner	**jantar** *zsuhn•tahr*
What are your plans for…?	**Quais são os seus planos para…?** *kweyez sohm ooz sehooz pluh•nooz puh•ruh…*
tonight	**hoje à noite** *auzseh ah noyt*
tomorrow	**amanhã** *uh•muh•nyuh*
this weekend	**este fim de semana** *ehst feeng deh seh•muh•nuh*
Where would you like to go?	**Onde queres ir?** *aund kehrz eer*
I'd like to go to…	**Quero ir à…** *keh•roo eer ah…*
Do you like…?	**Gosta de…?** *gaw•stuh deh…*
Can I have your number/e-mail?	**Podes dar-me o teu número de telefone/e-mail?** *pawd•ehz dahr•meh oo tehoo noo•meh•roo deh tehl•fawn /ee•mehl*
Are you on Facebook/Twitter?	**Está no Facebook/Twitter?** *ee•stah noo facebook/twitter*
Can I join you?	**Posso acompanhar-te?** *paw•soo uh•kaum•puh•nyahr•teh*
You look great!	**Está linda!** *ee•stah leen•duh*
Let's go somewhere quieter.	**Vamos para um sítio [lugar] mais sossegado.** *vuh•mooz puh•ruh oong see•tyoo [loo•gahr] meyez soo•seh•gah•thoo*

For Communications, see page 52.

Accepting & Rejecting

I'd love to.	**Adorava [adoraria] ir.** *uh•daw•rah•vuh [uh•doo•ruh•ree•uh] eer*

Where should we meet?	**Onde nos vamos encontrar?**	*aund nooz <u>vuh</u>•mooz ehng•kaun•<u>trahr</u>*
I'll meet you at the bar/ your hotel.	**Vou ter contigo [te encontrar] ao bar/hotel.**	*vauoo tehr kaun•<u>tee</u>•goo [tee ehn•kaun•<u>trahr</u>] ahoo bahr/<u>aw</u>•tehl*
I'll come by at…	**Eu passo por lá às…**	*ehoo <u>pah</u>•soo poor lah ahz…*
What's your address?	**Qual é a sua morada [endereço]?**	*kwahl eh uh <u>soo</u>•uh maw•<u>rah</u>•duh [ehn•deh•<u>reh</u>•soo]*
I'm busy.	**Mas tenho imenso [muito] que fazer.**	*muhz <u>teh</u>•nyoo ee•<u>mehn</u>•soo [<u>mooee</u>•too] keh fuh•<u>zehr</u>*
I'm not interested.	**Não estou interessado *m*/interessada *f*.**	*nohm ee•<u>stawoo</u> een•treh•<u>sah</u>•thoo/een•treh•<u>sah</u>•thuh*
Leave me alone.	**Deixe-me em paz.**	*<u>day</u>•sheh•meh eng pahz*
Stop bothering me!	**Está quieto!**	*ee•<u>stah</u> kee•<u>eh</u>•too*

Getting Intimate

Can I hug/kiss you?	**Posso [te] dar-te um abraço/beijo?**	*<u>paw</u>•soo [teh] <u>dahr</u>•teh oong uh•<u>brah</u>•soo/<u>bay</u>•zsoo*
Yes.	**Sim.**	*seeng*
No.	**Não.**	*nohm*
Stop!	**Pára!**	*<u>pah</u>•ruh*
I love you.	**Amo-te [Te amo].**	*<u>uh</u>•moo teh [teh <u>uh</u>•moo]*

Sexual Preferences

Are you gay?	**Ès homossexual?**	*ehz aw•maw•<u>sehk</u>•soo•ahl*
I'm…	**Sou…**	*sauoo…*
heterosexual	**heterossexual**	*eh•teh•raw•<u>sehk</u>•soo•ahl*
homosexual	**homossexual**	*aw•maw•<u>sehk</u>•soo•ahl*
bisexual	**bissexual**	*bee•<u>sehk</u>•soo•ahl*
Do you like men/women?	**Gosta de homens/mulheres?**	*<u>gaw</u>•stuh deh <u>aw</u>•mengz/moo•<u>lyehrz</u>*

For Grammar, see page 169.

113

Leisure Time

ESSENTIAL

Where's the tourist office?	**Onde é o posto de turismo [informações turísticas]?** *aund eh oo pau•stoo deh too•reez•moo [een•foor•muh•soings too•ree•stee•kuhz]*
What are the main points of interest?	**O que há de mais interessante para se ver?** *oo kee ah deh meyez een•tehr•reh•suhnt puh•ruh seh vehr*
Do you have tours in English?	**Tem excursões em inglês?** *teng ee•skoor•soings eng eng•lehz*
Can I have a map/guide?	**Pode dar-me um mapa/guia?** *pawd dahr•meh oong mah•puh/ gee•uh*

Tourist Information

Do you have any information on...?	**Tem informação sobre...?** *teng een•foor•muh•sohm sau•breh...*
Can you recommend...?	**Pode recomendar-me...?** *pawd reh•koo•mehn•dahr•meh...*
a boat trip	**uma excursão de barco** *oo•muh ee•skoor•sohm deh bahr•koo*
an excursion	**uma excursão** *oo•muh ee•skoor•sohm*
a sightseeing tour	**um circuito turístico** *oong seer•koo•ee•too too•ree•stee•koo*

In Brazil and Portugal, town maps and brochures on main tourist attractions are available at airports and from tourist information centers. Ask at your hotel or check online to find the nearest office.

On Tour

I'd like to go on the tour to…	**Gostaria de ir na excursão para…** *goo•stuh•<u>ree</u>•uh deh eer nuh ee•skoor•<u>sohm</u> puh•ruh…*
When's the next tour?	**Quando é a próxima excursão?** *kwuhn•doo eh uh <u>praw</u>•see•muh ee•skoor•<u>sohm</u>*
Are there tours in English?	**Há excursões em inglês?** *ah ee•skoor•<u>soings</u> eng eeng•<u>lehz</u>*
Is there an English-speaking guide/audio guide?	**Há algum guia que fale inglês/uma gravação da visita guiada em inglês?** *ah ahl•<u>goong</u> <u>gee</u>•uh keh <u>fah</u>•leh eeng•<u>lehz</u>/<u>oo</u>•muh gruh•vuh•<u>sohm</u> deh vee•<u>zee</u>•tuh gee•<u>ah</u>•duh eng eeng•<u>lehz</u>*
What time do we leave/return?	**Quando saímos/regressemos?** *kwuhn•doo suh•<u>eemooz</u>/reh•<u>greh</u>•seh•mooz*
We'd like to see…	**Gostaríamos de ver…** *goo•stuh•<u>ree</u>•uh•mooz deh vehr…*
Can we stop here…?	**Podemos parar aqui…?** *poo•<u>deh</u>•mooz puh•<u>rahr</u> uh•<u>kee</u>…*
to take photographs	**para tirar fotografias** *puh•ruh tee•<u>rahr</u> foo•too•gruh•<u>fee</u>•uhz*
to buy souvenirs	**para comprar lembranças** *puh•ruh kaum•<u>prahr</u> leng•<u>bruhn</u>•suhz*

| to use the restrooms [toilets] | **para usar as casas de banho [os banheiros]** *puh•ruh oo•zahr uhz kah•zuhz deh buh•nyoo [ooz buh•nyay•rooz]* |
| Is there access for the disabled? | **Há algum acesso para os deficientes?** *ah ahl•goong uh•seh•soo puh•ruh ooz deh•fee•see•ehntz* |

For Tickets, see page 20.

For Disabled Travelers, see page 153.

Seeing the Sights

Where is/are…?	**Onde é/são…?** *aund eh/sohm…*
the battleground	**o campo de batalha** *oo kuhm•poo deh buh•tah•lyuh*
the botanical garden	**o jardim botânico** *oo zsuhr•deeng boo•tuh•nee•koo*
the castle	**o castelo** *oo kuhz•teh•loo*
the downtown area	**o centro da cidade** *oo sehn•troo duh see•dahd*
the fountain	**a fonte** *uh faun•teh*
the library	**a biblioteca** *uh bee•blee•aw•teh•kuh*
the market	**o mercado** *oo mehr•kah•doo*
the museum	**o museu** *oo moo•zehoo*
the old town	**a parte velha da cidade** *uh pahrt veh•lyuh duh see•dahd*
the palace	**o palácio** *oo puh•lah•see•yoo*
the park	**o parque** *oo pahr•keh*
the ruins	**as ruínas** *uhz roo•een•uhz*
the shopping area	**a zona comercial** *uh zau•nuh koo•mehr•see•ahl*
the town square	**a praça central** *uh prah•suh sehn•trahl*
Can you show me on the map?	**Pode indicar-me no mapa?** *pawd een•dee•kahr•meh noo mah•puh*

It's...	É... *eh...*
amazing	**espantoso** *ee·spuhn·tau·zoo*
beautiful	**lindo** *leen·doo*
boring	**aborrecido** *uh·boo·rreh·see·thoo*
interesting	**interessante** *een·teh·reh·suhnt*
magnificent	**magnífico** *mahg·nee·fee·koo*
romantic	**romântico** *roo·muhn·tee·koo*
strange	**estranho** *ee·struh·nyoo*
stunning	**estupendo** *ee·stoo·pehn·doo*
terrible	**horrível** *aw·rree·vehl*
ugly	**feio** *fay·oo*
I (don't) like any of it.	**(Não) gosto de tudo.** *(nohm) gaw·stoo deh too·tho*

For Asking Directions, see page 36.

Religious Sites

Where's...?	**Onde é...?** *aund eh...*
the cathedral	**a catedral** *uh keh·teh·drahl*
the Catholic/ Protestant church	**a igreja católica/protestante** *uh ee·gray·zsuh kuh·taw·lee·kuh/praw·tee·stuhnt*
the mosque	**a mesquita** *uh mehz·kee·tuh*
Where's...?	**Onde é...?** *aund eh...*
the shrine	**o relicário** *oo reh·lee·kah·ree·oo*
the synagogue	**a sinagoga** *uh seen·uh·gaw·guh*
the temple	**o templo** *oo tehm·ploo*
What time is mass/ the service?	**A que horas é a missa/o culto?** *uh kee aw·ruhz eh uh mee·suh/oo kool·too*

118

Shopping

ESSENTIAL

Where is the market/mall [shopping?	**Onde é o mercado/o centro comercial?** *aund eh oo mehr•kah•thoo/oo sehn•troo koo•mehr•see•ahl*
I'm just looking.	**Estou só a ver [vendo].** *ee•stawoo saw uh vehr [vehn•doo]*
Can you help me?	**Pode ajudar-me?** *pawd uh•zsoo•dahr•meh*
I'm being helped.	**Alguém está a [me] ajudar-me.** *ahl•gehng ee•stah uh [meh] uh•zsoo•dahr•meh*
How much is it?	**Quanto é?** *kwuhn•too eh*
That one, please.	**Aquele m/Aquela f, por favor.** *uh•kehl/uh•keh•luh poor fuh•vaur*
That's all, thanks.	**É tudo, obrigado m/obrigada f.** *eh too•doo aw•bree•gah•doo/aw•bree•gah•thuh*
Where can I pay?	**Onde pago?** *aund pah•goo*
I'll pay in cash/by credit card.	**Pago com dinheiro/com o cartão de crédito.** *pah•goo kaum dee•nyay•roo/kaum oo kuhr•tohm deh kreh•dee•too*
A receipt, please.	**Um recibo, se faz favor.** *oong reh•see•boo seh fahz fuh•vaur*

Flea markets in Portugal are common in almost every town and
usually occur once a week or every other week (in smaller towns).
These are the best places to get the most for your money. Haggling
is common and almost expected. It is rare to pay full price for anything
except food, for which prices are generally not negotiable. Bring cash,
as few vendors accept credit cards.

At the Shops

Where is/are...?	**Onde é/são...?** *aund eh/sohm...*
the antiques store	**a loja das antiguidades** *uh law·zsuh duhz uhn·tee·gee·dah·dehz*
the bakery	**a padaria** *uh pah·deh·ree·uh*
the bank	**o banco** *oo buhn·koo*
the bookstore	**a livraria** *uh lee·vreh·ree·uh*
the clothing store	**a loja de artigos de vestuário** *uh law·zsuh deh uhr·tee·gooz de veh·stoo·ah·ree·oo*
the delicatessen	**a charcutaria** *uh shuhr·koo·tuh·ree·uh*
the department store	**o grande armazém [a loja de departamentos]** *oo gruhnd uhr·muh·zeng [uh law·zsuh deh deh·puhr·tuh·mehn·tooz]*
the gift shop	**a loja de recordações** *uh law·zsuh deh reh·kaur·duh·soingz*
the health food store	**a loja de produtos dietéticos** *uh law·zsuh deh proo·doo·tooz dee·eh·tee·kooz*
the jeweler	**a joalharia [joalheria]** *uh zsoo·uh·lyuh·ree·uh [zsoo·uh·lyeh·ree·uh]*
the liquor store [off-licence]	**a loja de vinhos** *uh law·zsuh deh vee·nyooz*
the market	**o mercado** *oo mehr·kah·doo*

the music store	**a loja de música**	*uh law•zsuh deh moo•zee•cuh*
Where is/are...?	**Onde é/são...?**	*aund eh/sohm...*
the pastry shop	**a pastelaria [confeitaria]**	*uh puh•stuh•luh•ree•uh [kaun•fay•tuh•ree•uh]*
the pharmacy [chemist]	**a farmácia**	*uh fuhr•mah•see•uh*
the produce [grocery] store	**a frutaria [quitanda]**	*uh froo•tuh•ree•uh [kee•tuhn•duh]*
the shoe store	**a sapataria**	*uh suh•puh•tuh•ree•uh*
the shopping mall [shopping centre]	**o centro comercial**	*oo sehn•troo koo•mehr•see•ahl*
the souvenir store	**a loja de lembranças**	*uh law•zsuh deh lehn•bruhn•suhz*
the supermarket	**o supermercado**	*oo soo•pehr•mehr•kah•thoo*
the tobacconist	**a tabacaria**	*uh tuh•bah•kuh•ree•uh*
the toy store	**o armazém [a loja] de brinquedos**	*oo ahr•muh•zehn [uh law•zsuh] deh breeng•keh•dooz*

Ask an Assistant

What are the opening hours?	**Qual a hora de abertura?**	*kwahl uh aw•ruh deh ah•behr•too•ruh*
Where is/are...?	**Onde é/são...?**	*aund eh/sohm...*
the cashier	**a caixa**	*uh keye•shuh*
the escalator	**a escada rolante**	*uh ees•kah•duh roo•luhnt*
the elevator [lift]	**o elevador**	*oo eh•leh•vuh•daur*
the fitting room	**os vestiários**	*ooz vehs•tee•ah•ree•ooz*
the store directory [guide]	**a planta da loja**	*uh pluhn•tuh duh law•zsuh*
Can you help me?	**Pode ajudar-me?**	*pawd uh•zsoo•dahr•meh*
I'm just looking.	**Estou só a ver [vendo].**	*ee•stawoo saw uh vehr [vehn•doo]*

I'm being helped.	**Alguém está a [me] ajudar-me.** *ahl•geng ee•stah uh [meh] uh•zsoo•dahr•meh*	
Do you have…?	**Tem…?** *teng…*	
Could you show me…?	**Podia mostrar-me…?** *poo•dee•uh mooz•trahr•meh…*	
Can you ship it /wrap it ?	**Pode despachá-lo/embrulhá-lo?** *pawd dehs•puh•shah•loo/eng•broo•lyah•loo*	
How much is it?	**Quanto é?** *kwuhn•too eh*	
That's all, thanks.	**É tudo, obrigado** *m* /**obrigada** *f.* *eh too•doo aw•bree•gah•doo/aw•bree•gah•duh*	

For Clothing, see page 127.

For Meals & Cooking, see page 71.

For Souvenirs, see page 133.

YOU MAY HEAR…

Deseja alguma coisa? *deh•zay•zuh ahl•goo•muh koy•zuh*	Would you like something?
Um momento. *oong moo•mehn•too*	One moment.
O que é que deseja? *oo kee eh keh deh•zay•zsuh*	What would you like?
Mais alguma coisa? *meyez ahl•goo•muh koy•zuh*	Anything else?

YOU MAY SEE…

HORÁRIO DE ABERTURA	opening hours
FECHADO PARA ALMOÇO	closed for lunch
PROVADOR	fitting room
CAIXA	cashier
SÓ DINHEIRO	cash only
CARTÕES DE CRÉDITO ACEITES	credit cards accepted

Personal Preferences

I'd like something…	**Queria uma coisa…**	keh•_ree_•uh _oo_•muh _koy_•zuh…
cheap/expensive	**barata/cara**	buh•_rah_•tuh/_kah_•ruh
larger/smaller	**maior/mais pequena [menor]**	meye•_awr_/meyez peh•_keh_•nuh [_mee_•nawr]
from this region	**desta região**	_dehs_•tuh ree•zsee•_ohm_
Around… euros.	**Cerca de… euros.**	_sehr_•ka deh… ehoo•rooz
Is it real?	**É verdadeiro?**	eh vehr•duh•_day_•roo
Could you show me this/that ?	**Podia mostrar-me este/esse?**	poo•_dee_•uh moos•_trahr_•meh ehst/ehs
That's not quite what I want.	**Não é bem o que quero.**	nohm eh beng oo keh _keh_•roo
No, I don't like it.	**Não, não gosto.**	nohm nohm _gaw_•stoo
It's too expensive.	**É caro demais.**	eh _kah_•roo deh•_meyez_
I have to think about it.	**Tenho que pensar nisto.**	_tay_•nyoo keh pehn•_sahr nee_•stoo
I'll take it.	**Levo.**	_leh_•voo

Paying & Bargaining

How much?	**Quanto é?**	_kwuhn_•too eh
I'll pay…	**Pago…**	_pah_•goo…
in cash	**com dinheiro**	kaum dee•_nyay_•roo
by credit card	**com o cartão de crédito**	kaum oo kuhr•_tohm_ deh _kreh_•dee•too
by traveler's check [cheque]	**com livro de cheques**	kaum _lee_•vroo deh _sheh_•kehz
A receipt, please.	**Um recibo, se faz favor.**	oong reh•_see_•boo seh fahz fuh•_vaur_
That's too much.	**Isso é muito.**	_ee_•soo eh _mooee_•too
I'll give you…	**Vou dar-lhe…**	vau _dahr_•lyeh…
I only have…euros/reais.	**Só tenho…euros/reais.**	saw _teh_•nyoo… _eeoo_•rooz/rree•_eyez_

Is that your best price?

É o preço melhor que me pode dar? *eh oo preh•soo mee•lyawr keh meh pawd dahr*

Can you give me a discount?

Pode-me dar um desconto? *pawd•meh dahr oong dehs•kaun•too*

For Numbers, see page 173.

In Portugal and Brazil, international credit cards are generally accepted. The most commonly used cards are Visa™, American Express®, Europay/Mastercard™, JCB and Maestro®. In some small villages and towns cash may still be the only form of currency accepted.

YOU MAY HEAR...

Como deseja pagar? *kau•moo deh•zay•zsuh puh•gahr*

How are you paying?

Esta transacção não foi autorizada. *eh•stuh truhn•suh•sohm nohm foy ahoo•too•ree•zah•thuh*

This transaction was not authorized.

Não aceitamos cartões de crédito. *nohm uh•say•tuh•mooz kuhr•toings deh kreh•dee•too*

We don't accept credit cards.

Só com dinheiro, por favor. *saw kaum dee•nyay•roo poor fuh•vaur*

Cash only, please.

Não tem troco [trocado]? *nohm teng trau•koo [trau•kah•doo]*

Do you have any smaller bills?

A identificação, por favor. *uh ee•dehnt•tee•fee•kuh•sohm, poor fuh•vaur*

ID, please.

Making a Complaint

I'd like…	**Queria…** *keh•ree•uh…*
to exchange this	**trocar isto** *troo•kahr ee•stoo*
to return this	**retornar isto** *ree•tawrr•nahr ee•stoo*
a refund	**um reembolso** *oong ree•eng•baul•soo*
to see the manager	**falar com o gerente** *m* **/a gerente** *f fuh•lahr kaum oo zseh•rehnt/uh zseh•rehnt*

Services

Can you recommend…?	**Pode recomendar-me…?** *pawd reh•koo•mehn•dahr•meh…*
a barber	**o cabeleireiro de homens** *oo kuh•beh•lay•ray•roo deh aw•mengs*
a dry cleaner	**a lavandaria de limpeza a seco** *uh luh•vuhn•duh•ree•uh deh leeng•peh•zuh uh seh•koo*
a hairdresser	**o cabeleireiro de senhoras** *oo kuh•beh•lay•ray•roo deh see•nyau•ruhz*
a laundromat [launderette]	**a lavandaria [lavanderia]** *uh luh•vuhn•duh•ree•uh [uh luh•vuhn•deh•ree•uh]*
a nail salon	**o salão das unhas** *oo suh•lohm duhz oo•nyuhz*
a spa	**o spa** *oo spa*
a travel agency	**a agência de viagens** *uh ah•zsehn•see•uh deh vee•ah•zsengs*
Can you…this?	**Pode…isto?** *pawd…ee•stoo*
alter	**modificar** *moo•dee•fee•kahr*
clean	**limpar** *leem•parh*
mend	**consertar** *kaun•sehr•tahr*
press	**engomar** *eeng•goo•mahr*
When will it be ready?	**Quando estará pronto?** *kwuhn•doo ee•stuh•rah praun•too*

Hair & Beauty

I'd like…	**Queria…** keh•*ree*•uh…
an appointment for	**fazer uma marcação [marcar um horário]**
today/tomorrow	**para hoje/amanhã** fuh•*zehr* oo•muh mahr•kuh•*sohm* [muhr•*kahr* oong aw•*rah*•ree•oo] puh•ruh auzeh/uh•muh•*nyuh*
some color	**alguma cor** ahl•*goo*•muh kaur
some highlights	**madeixas** muh•*day*•shuhz
my hair styled/ blow-dried	**meu cabelo penteado/seco com secador** mehoo kuh•*beh*•loo pehn•tee•*ah*•thoo/seh•koo kaum seh•kuh•daur
a haircut	**um corte** oong kawrt
a trim	**acertar as pontas [aparar]** uh•sehr•*tahr* uhz *paun*•tuhz [uh•puh•*rahr*]
Don't cut it too short.	**Não corte muito curto.** nohm kawrt *mooee*•too *koor*•too
Shorter here.	**Mais curto aqui.** meyez *koor*•too uh•*kee*
I'd like…	**Queria…** keh•*ree*•uh…
an eyebrow/ a bikini wax	**uma cera de sobrancelha/biquíni** *oo*•muh *seh*•ruh deh sau•bruhn•*seh*•lyuhz/ bee•*kee*•nee
I'd like…	**Queria…** keh•*ree*•uh…
a facial	**uma limpeza de pele** *oo*•muh leem•*peh*•zuh deh *pehl*
a manicure/pedicure	**uma manicure/um pedicure** *oo*•muh muh•nee•*koor*/oong peh•dee•*koor*
a (sports) massage	**uma massagem (desportiva [esportiva])** *oo*•muh mehn•*sah*•zseng (dee•*spawr*•tee•vuh [ee•*spawr*•tee•vuh])
Do you do…?	**Faz…?** fahz…
acupuncture	**acupuntura** uh•koo•poon•*too*•ruh

aromatherapy	**aromaterapia** uh·raw·muh·teh·reh·_pee_·uh
oxygen treatment	**tratamento de oxigénio** truh·tuh·_mehn_·too deh awk·see·_zseh_·nee·oo
Is there a sauna?	**Há sauna?** ah _sahoo_·nuh

Portugal is well-known for the benefits of its natural mineral waters and offers many healing and wellness centers. Contact the **Associação das Termas de Portugal** (Association of Facilities of Portugal) for a list of centers throughout Portugal.
In Portugal and Brazil, check with your hotel concierge for information on local spas that offer massage, acupuncture and skin treatments. These spas are most often found in large cities. The service fee is usually included in the price, but an additional 10% tip is appreciated for extraordinary service.

Antiques

How old is this?	**Qual é a data disto?** kwahl eh uh _dah_·tuh _dee_·stoo
Do you have anything from the…period?	**Tem alguma coisa do período…?** teng ahl·_goo_·muh _koy_·zuh thoo peh·ree·_oo_·thoo…
Do I have to fill out any forms?	**Tenho que completar algum formulário?** teh·nyoo keh kaum·pleh·_tahr_ ahl·_goom_ fawr·moo·_lah_·ree·oo
Is there a certificate of authenticity?	**Há um certificado de autenticidade?** ah oong sehr·tee·fee·_kah_·thoo deh aw·tehn·tee·see·_dahd_
Can you ship/wrap it?	**Pode enviar/embrulhar?** pawd ehn·vee·ahr/ ehm·broo·lyahr

Clothing

| I'd like… | **Queria…** keh·_ree_·uh… |
| Can I try this on? | **Posso provar isto?** _paw_·soo proo·_vahr_ ee·stoo |

It doesn't fit.	**Não me serve.** *nohm meh sehrv*
It's too…	**É muito…** *eh mooee•too…*
big	**grande** *grawnd*
small	**pequeno** *m* /**pequena** *f peh•kehn•oo/peh•kehn•uh*
short	**curto** *m* /**curta** *f koor•too/koor•tuh*
long	**comprido** *m* /**comprida** *f kaum•pree•doo/ kaum•pree•duh*
tight/loose	**justo/largo** *zsooz•too/lahr•goo*
Do you have this in size…?	**Tem isto no tamanho…?** *teng ee•stoo noo tuh•muh•nyoo…*
Do you have this in a bigger/smaller size?	**Tem isto num tamanho maior/mais pequeno [menor]?** *teng ee•stoo noong tuh•muh•nyoo meye•awr/meyez peh•kehn•oo[mee•nor]*

For Numbers, see page 173.

YOU MAY HEAR…

Isso fica-lhe bem. *ee•soo fee•kuh•lyeh beng*	That looks great on you.
Como é que fica? *kau•moo eh keh fee•kuh*	How does it fit?
Não temos o seu tamanho. *nohm teh•mooz oo sehoo tuh•muh•nyoo*	We don't have your size.

YOU MAY SEE…

ROUPA DE HOMEM	men's clothing
ROUPA DE SENHORA	women's clothing
ROUPA DE CRIANÇAS	children's clothing

Colors

I'd like something…	**Queria algo…** keh·*ree*·uh *ahl*·goo…
beige	**em beige [bege]** eng *bay*·zseh [*bay*·zseh]
black	**em preto** eng *preh*·too
blue	**em azul** eng uh·*zool*
brown	**em castanho [marrom]** eng kuhz·*tay*·nyoo [muh·*rraum*]
green	**em verde** eng vehrd
gray	**em cinzento [cinza]** eng seeng·*zehn*·too [*seen*·zuh]
orange	**em cor-de-laranja** eng kaur deh luh·*ruhn*·zsuh
pink	**em cor-de-rosa** eng kaur deh *raw*·zuh
purple	**em roxo** eng *rau*·shoo
red	**em vermelho** eng vehr·*meh*·lyoo
white	**em branco** eng *bruhn*·koo
yellow	**em amarelo** eng uh·meh·*reh*·loo

Clothes & Accessories

backpack	**a mochila** uh moo·*shee*·luh
belt	**o cinto** oo *seen*·too
bikini	**o bikini [biquini]** oo bee·*kee*·nee [bee·*kee*·nee]
blouse	**a blusa** uh *bloo*·zuh
bra	**o soutien [sutiã]** oo soot·ee·*ehn* [soo·tee·*uh*]
briefs [underpants]	**as calcinhas** uhz kahl·*see*·nyuhz
coat	**o casaco comprido** oo kuh·*zah*·koo kaum·*pree*·thoo
dress	**o vestido** oo vehs·*tee*·thoo
hat	**o chapéu** oo shuh·*pehoo*
jacket	**o casaco curto** oo kuh·*zah*·koo *koor*·too
jeans	**as calças de ganga** uhz *kahl*·suhz deh *guhn*·guh
pants [trousers]	**as calças** uhz *kahl*·suhz
pantyhose [tights]	**o collant** oo koo·*luhnt*

purse [handbag]	**a mala de mão [bolsa]** uh _mah_•luh deh mohm [_baul_•sah]
raincoat	**a gabardine** uh guh•buhr•_deen_
scarf	**o lenço de pescoço** oo _lehn_•soo deh pehz•_kau_•soo
shirt	**a camisa** uh kuh•_mee_•zuh
shorts	**os calções** ooz kahl•_soingz_
skirt	**a saia** uh _seye_•uh
socks	**as peúgas [meias curtas]** uhz peh•_oo_•guhz [_may_•uhz _koor_•tuhz]
suit	**o fato [terno]** oo _fah_•too [_tehr_•noo]
sunglasses	**os óculos de sol** ooz _aw_•koo•looz deh sawl
sweater	**a camisola [o suéter]** uh kuh•mee•_zaw_•luh [oo _sweh_•tur]
sweatshirt	**o sweatshirt [a blusa de moleton]** oo _sweht_•shur [uh _bloo_•zuh deh mool•ee•_tawn_]
swimming trunks	**os calções de banho** ooz kahl•_soingz_ deh _buh_•nyoo
swimsuit	**o fato [maiô] de banho** oo _fah_•too [meye•_au_] deh _buh_•nyoo
T-shirt	**a camiseta/T-shirt** uh kuh•mee•_seh_•tuh/_tee_•shurt
tie	**gravata** gruh•_vah_•tuh
underwear	**roupa interior** _rau_•puh eeng•teh•ree•_aur_

Fabric

I'd like…	**Queria…** *keh•ree•uh…*	
cotton	**algodão** *ahl•goo•dohm*	
denim	**ganga [brim]** *guhn•guh [breeng]*	
lace	**renda** *rehn•duh*	
leather	**cabedal [couro]** *kuh•beh•dahl [kau•roo]*	
linen	**linho** *lee•nyoo*	
silk	**seda** *seh•thuh*	
wool	**lã** *luh*	
Is it machine washable?	**Isto é para lavar na máquina?** *ee•stoo eh puh•ruh luh•vahr nuh mah•kee•nuh*	

Shoes

I'd like a pair of…	**Queria um par de…** *keh•ree•uh oong pahr deh…*
high-heeled/ flat shoes	**sapatos altos/baixos** *suh•pah•tooz ahl•tooz/ beye•shooz*
boots	**botas** *baw•tuhz*
loafers	**mandriões** *muhn•dree•oingz*
sandals	**sandálias** *suhn•dah•lee•uhz*
shoes	**sapatos** *suh•pah•tooz*
slippers	**chinelas [pantufas]** *shee•neh•luhz [puhn•too•fuhz]*
sneakers	**sapatos de ténis [tênis]** *suh•pah•tooz deh teh•neez [tehn•ehz]*
In size…	**No tamanho…** *noo tuh•muh•nyoo…*

For Numbers, see page 173.

Sizes

small (S)	**pequeno** *peh•keh•noo*	
medium (M)	**medio** *meh•dee•oo*	
large (L)	**grande** *gruhnd*	
extra large (XL)	**extra grande** *ay•struh gruhnd*	

| petite | **pequeno** _peh•keh•noo_ |
| plus size | **tamanho de factor positivo** _tuh•muh•nyoo deh_ _fah•taur poo•see•tee•voo_ |

Newsagent & Tobacconist

Do you sell English-language newspapers?	**Vende jornais em inglês?** _vehn•deh zsoor•neyez eng eeng•lehz_
I'd like...	**Queria...** _keh•ree•uh..._
candy [sweets]	**rebuçados [balas]** _reh•boo•sah•dooz [bah•luhz]_
chewing gum	**uma pastilha elástica [goma de mascar]** _oo•muh puhz•tee•lyuh ee•lah•stee•kuh [gau•muh deh muhz•kahr]_
a chocolate bar	**um chocolate** _oong shoo•koo•lah•teh_
a cigar	**um charuto** _oong shuh•roo•too_
I'd like...	**Queria...** _keh•ree•uh..._
a pack/carton of cigarettes	**um maço/pacote de cigarros** _oong mah•soo/ puh•kaut deh see•gah•rrooz_
a lighter	**um isqueiro** _oong ees•kay•roo_
a magazine	**uma revista** _oo•muh reh•vee•stuh_
matches	**fósforos** _fawz•fuh•rooz_
a newspaper	**um jornal** _oong zsoorr•nahl_
a pen	**uma caneta** _oo•muh kuh•neh•tuh_
a postcard	**um postal** _oong poo•stahl_
a road/town map of...	**um mapa de/da cidade de...** _oong mah•puh deh/deh see•dahd deh..._
stamps	**selos** _seh•looz_

Photography

| I'm looking for...camera. | **Estou à procura de [procurando] uma máquina fotográfica...** _ee•stawoo ah praw•koo•ruh deh [praw•koo•ruhn•doo] oo•muh mah•kee•nuh faw•too•grah•fee•kuh..._ |

an automatic	**automática** _ahoo•too•<u>mah</u>•tee•kuh_	
a digital	**digital** _deh•zseh•<u>tahl</u>_	
a disposable	**descartável** _dehz•kuhr•<u>tah</u>•vehl_	
I'd like...	**Queria...** _keh•<u>ree</u>•uh..._	
a battery	**uma pilha** <u>oo</u>•muh <u>pee</u>•lyuh	
digital prints	**impressões digitais** _eem•preh•<u>soingz</u>_ _deh•zseh•<u>teyez</u>_	
a memory card	**um cartão de memória** _oong kuhr•<u>tohm</u> deh_ _meh•<u>maw</u>•ree•uh_	

Can I print digital photos here? **Posso imprimir fotos digitais aqui?** _<u>paw</u>•soo eem•pree•<u>meer</u> <u>faw</u>•tooz deh•zeh•<u>teyez</u> uh•<u>kee</u>_

Souvenirs

bottle of wine	**a garrafa de vinho** _uh guh•<u>rrah</u>•fuh deh <u>vee</u>•nyoo_
box of chocolates	**a caixa de chocolates** _uh <u>keye</u>•shuh deh shoo•koo•<u>lah</u>•tehz_
calendar	**o calendário** _oo kuh•lehn•<u>dah</u>•ree•oo_
postcards	**postais** _pooz•<u>teyez</u>_
scarf	**o lenço** _oo <u>lehn</u>•soo_
souvenir guide	**o guia turístico** _oo <u>gee</u>•uh too•<u>ree</u>•stee•koo_
T-shirt	**a camiseta** _uh kuh•mee•<u>seh</u>•tuh_
toy/game	**o brinquedo/jogo** _oo breeng•<u>keh</u>•thoo/<u>zsaw</u>•goo_
wine	**o vinho** _oo <u>vee</u>•nyoo_
Can I see this/that?	**Posso ver este/esse?** _<u>paw</u>•soo vehr ehst/eh•seh_
It's the one in the window/display case.	**É aquele na janela/montra.** _eh uh•<u>kehl</u> nuh zsuh•<u>neh</u>•luh/<u>mau</u>•ntruh_
I'd like...	**Queria...** _keh•<u>ree</u>•uh..._
a battery	**uma pilha** <u>oo</u>•muh <u>pee</u>•lyuh
a bracelet	**uma pulseira** <u>oo</u>•muh pool•<u>say</u>•ruh
a brooch	**um broche** _oong brawsh_
earrings	**uns brincos** _oongs <u>breeng</u>•kooz_

a necklace	**um colar** *oong koo-lahr*
a ring	**um anel** *oong uh-nehl*
a watch	**um relógio de pulso** *oong reh-loy-zsoo deh pool-soo*
copper	**cobre** *kaw-breh*
crystal	**cristal** *kree-stahl*
diamonds	**brilhantes** *bree-lyuhntz*
white/yellow gold	**ouro branco/amarelo** *au-roo bruhn-koo/ uh-muh-reh-loo*
pearls	**pérolas** *peh-roo-luhz*
pewter	**peltre** *pehl-treh*
platinum	**platina** *plah-tee-nuh*
sterling silver	**prata** *prah-tuh*
Is this real?	**É verdadeiro?** *eh vehr-duh-day-roo*
Can you engrave it?	**Pode gravá-lo?** *pawd gruh-vah-loo*

Souvenirs you might want to take home from Portugal include pottery, leather goods, tiles and copperware, especially the famous **cataplana**. Wooden painted roosters (**galos de barcelos**) also make great souvenirs as they are a national symbol. And don't forget some of the famous **Vinho do Porto**, Port wine.

Popular Brazilian souvenirs include antique furniture, baskets, coffee, dolls in regional costumes, embroidery, Indian crafts, jacaranda-wood salad bowls and trays and tapestries.

Afro-Brazilian musical instruments provide alternative ideas as presents. Some examples are **berimbau** (stretched metal strip, played with a stick), **bongô** (bongo drums) and **atabaque** (another type of drum).

Sport & Leisure

ESSENTIAL

When's the game?	**Quando é o jogo?** <u>kwuhn</u>•doo eh o <u>zsau</u>•goo
Where's…?	**Onde é…?** aund eh…
the beach	**a praia** uh <u>preye</u>•uh
the park	**o parque** oo <u>pahr</u>•keh
the pool	**a piscina** uh pee•<u>see</u>•nuh
Is it safe to swim here?	**Pode-se nadar aqui sem perigo?** pawd seh nuh•<u>dahr</u> uh•<u>kee</u> sehn peh•<u>ree</u>•goo
Can I hire golf clubs?	**Posso alugar tacos?** <u>paw</u>•soo uh•loo•<u>gahr</u> tah•kooz
How much per hour?	**Qual é a tarifa por hora?** kwahl eh uh tuh•<u>ree</u>•fuh poor <u>aw</u>•ruh
How far is it to…?	**A que distância fica…?** uh keh dee•<u>stuhn</u>•see•uh <u>fee</u>•kuh…
Can you show me on the map?	**Pode indicar-me no mapa?** pawd een•dee•<u>kahr</u>•meh noo <u>mah</u>•puh

Watching Sport

When's...?	**Quando é...?** _kwuhn•doo eh..._
the basketball game	**o jogo de basquetebol** _oo zsau•goo deh bah•skeht•bawl_
the boxing match	**a partida de boxe** _uh puhr•tee•duh deh bawkz_
the cycling race	**a corrida de bicicleta** _uh koo•ree•thuh deh bee•see•kleht_
the golf tournament	**o torneio de golfe** _oo taur•nay•oo deh gawlf_
the soccer [football] game	**o jogo de futebol** _oo zsau•goo deh foo•teh•bawl_
When's...?	**Quando é...?** _kwuhn•doo eh..._
the basketball game	**o jogo de basquetebol** _oo zsau•goo deh bah•skeht•bawl_
the tennis match	**a partida de ténis** _uh puhr•tee•thuh de teh•neez_
the volleyball game	**o jogo de voleibol** _oo zsau•goo deh vaw•lay•bawl_
Which teams are playing?	**Quais são as equipas [os times] que jogam?** _kweyez sohm uhz ee•kee•puhz [ooz tee•mehs] keh zsau•gohm_
Where's...?	**Onde é...?** _aund eh..._
the horsetrack	**a pista de cavalo** _uh peez•tuh deh kuh•vah•loo_
the racetrack	**o hipódromo** _oo ee•paw•drau•moo_
the stadium	**o pavilhão desportivo [esportivo]** _oo puh•vee•lyohm dehs•poor•tee•voo [ees•poor•tee•voo_
Where can I place a bet?	**Onde posso colocar uma aposta?** _aund paw•soo kaw•loo•kahr oo•muh uh•paws•tuh_

Portuguese and Brazilians are avid soccer fans. In Portugal, the teams Benfica, Porto and Sporting Lisbon attract huge crowds, while Rio boasts Maracanã, the largest soccer stadium in the world.

Playing Sport

Where's...?	**Onde é...?** *aund eh...*
the golf course	**o campo de golfe** *oo kuhm•poo deh gawlf*
the gym	**o clube desportivo [esportivo]** *oo kloob dehs•poor•tee•voo [ees•poor•tee•voo]*
the park	**o parque** *oo pahrk*
the tennis courts	**os campos [as quadras] de ténis** *ooz kuhm•pooz [uhz kwah•druhz] deh teh•neez*
How much per...?	**Qual é o preço por...?** *kwahl eh oo preh•soo poor...*
day	**dia** *dee•uh*
hour	**hora** *aw•ruh*
game	**jogo** *zsau•goo*
round	**volta** *vawl•tuh*
Can I rent [hire]...?	**Posso alugar...?** *paw•soo uh•loo•gahr...*
golf clubs	**tacos de golfe** *tah•kooz deh gawlf*
equipment	**o equipamento** *oo ee•kee•puh•mehn•too*
a racket	**uma raquete** *oo•muh rah•keht*

At the Beach/Pool

Where's the beach/pool?	**Onde é a praia/piscina?** *aund eh uh preye•uh/pee•see•nuh*
Is there...?	**Há...?** *ah...*
a kiddie pool	**uma piscina para crianças** *oo•muh pee•see•nuh puh•ruh kree•uhn•suhs*
an indoor/outdoor pool	**uma piscina coberta/ao ar livre** *oo•muh pee•see•nuh koo•behr•tuh/ahoo ahr lee•vreh*
a lifeguard	**uma salva-vidas** *oo•muh sahl•vuh vee•duhz*
Is it safe...?	**É perigoso...?** *eh per•ree•gau•zoo...*
to swim	**para nadar** *puh•ruh nuh•dahr*
to dive	**para mergulhar** *puh•ruh mehr•goo•lyahr*
for children	**para as crianças** *puh•ruh uhz kree•uhn•suhs*

I want to hire...	**Quero alugar...** _keh•roo uh•loo•gahr_...
a deck chair	**uma cadeira de encosto** _oo•muh kuh•day•ruh deh ehn•kaus•stoo_
diving equipment	**equipamento para mergulhar** _ee•kee•puh•mehn•too puh•ruh mehr•goo•lyahr_
a jet-ski	**um jet-ski** _oong zseht•skee_
a motorboat	**um barco a motor** _oong bahr•koo uh moo•taur_
a rowboat	**um barco a remos** _oong bahr•koo uh reh•mooz_
snorkling equipment	**equipamento de snorkling** _ee•kee•puh•mehn•too de snawr•kleeng_
a surfboard	**uma prancha de surf** _oo•muh pruhn•shuh deh soorf_
a towel	**uma toalha** _oo•muh too•ah•lyuh_
an umbrella	**um chapéu de sol [guarda sol]** _oong shuh•pehoo deh sol [gwahr•duh sawl]_
water skis	**esquis-aquáticos** _eez•keez uh•kwah•tee•kooz_
a windsurfer	**uma prancha à vela** _oo•muh pruhn•shuh ah veh•luh_
For...hours.	**Por...horas.** _poor... aw•ruhz_

For Traveling with Children, see page 150.

In Portugal, the **Algarve** has beautiful beaches, and the **Alentejo** (Atlantic Coast) is growing in popularity. Beaches in the north (**Caminha**, **Apúlia**, **Furadouro**) are good for surfing. Brazil is practically synonymous with beaches; **Copacabana** and **Ipanema** in Rio are known the world over. Surfing is popular all along the Brazilian coast, and beach volleyball is also a popular pursuit. In both Portugal and Brazil, the largest beaches have lifeguards, but look for the following swimming flags: red (swimming forbidden), yellow (swim near the beach), green (safe).

Winter Sports

A lift pass for a day/ five days, please.	**Uma passagem de esqui por um dia/cinco dias, por favor.** *oo•muh puh•sah•zseng deh ee•skee poor oong dee•uh/seeng•koo dee•uhz poor fuh•vaur*
I want to hire...	**Quero alugar...** *keh•roo uh•loo•gahr...*
boots	**botas** *baw•tuhz*
a helmet	**um capacete** *oong kuh•puh•seht*
poles	**polos** *pau•looz*
skis	**esquis** *ee•skeez*
a snowboard	**um snowboard** *oong sno•bawrd*
snowshoes	**sapatos de neve** *suh•pah•tooz deh nehv*
These are too big/small.	**Estes são muito grandes/pequenos.** *ehs•tehz sohm mooee•too gruhn•dehz/pee•keh•nooz*
Are there lessons?	**Há lições?** *ah lee•soingz*
I'm a beginner.	**Sou principiante.** *sawoo preen•see•puhnt*
I'm experienced.	**Tenho experiência.** *teh•nyoo ees•peh•ree•ehn•see•uh*
A trail [piste] map, please.	**Um mapa de trilha, por favor.** *oong mah•puh deh tree•lyuh poor fuh•vaur*

There is one place in Portugal with temperatures cold enough for skiing: **Serra da Estrela**, Portugal's highest mountain. Dress appropriately, as the weather at the bottom of the mountain (and the rest of Portugal) is not indicative of the freezing temperatures at the top of **Serra da Estrela**. It is not uncommon for temperatures to be thirty to fifty degrees colder at the top!

YOU MAY SEE...

LEVANTA DE ESQUI	drag lift
CARRO DE CABO/GANDOLA	cable car/gondola
CADEIRA LEVANTAMENTO	chair lift
NOVATO	novice
INTERMEDIÁRIO	intermediate
ESPECIALISTA	expert
PISTA FECHADA	trail [piste] closed

Out in the Country

I'd like a map...	**Queria um mapa...** keh·_ree_·uh oong _mah_·puh...
of this region	**desta região** _deh_·stuh reh·zsee·_ohm_
of the walking routes	**de itinerários a pé** deh ee·tee·neh·_rah_·ree·ooz a peh
of bike routes	**de itinerários de bicicleta** deh ee·tee·neh·_rah_·ree·ooz deh bee·see·_kleh_·tuh
of the trails	**dos caminhos** thooz kuh·_mee_·nyooz
Is it easy/difficult ?	**É fácil/difícil?** eh _fah_·seel/dee·_fee_·seel
Is it far/steep?	**É distante/precipício?** eh deez·_tuhnt_/pree·see·_pee_·see·oo
How far is it to...?	**A que distância fica...** uh keh dee·_stuhn_·see·uh _fee_·kuh...
Can you show me on the map?	**Pode indicar-me no mapa?** pawd een·dee·_kahr_·meh noo _mah_·puh
I'm lost.	**Estou perdido m /perdida f.** ee·_stawoo_ pehr·_dee_·doo/pehr·_dee_·duh
Where's...?	**Onde é...?** aund eh...
the bridge	**a ponte** uh paunt
the cave	**a caverna** uh kuh·_vehr_·nuh
the cliff	**a falésia** uh fuh·_leh_·see·uh

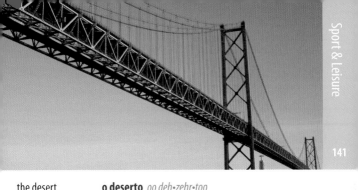

the desert	**o deserto** *oo deh·zehr·too*
the farm	**a quinta [fazenda]** *uh keen·tuh [fuh·zehn·dah]*
the field	**o campo** *oo kuhm·poo*
the forest	**a floresta** *uh flau·reh·stuh*
the hill	**a colina** *uh koo·lee·nuh*
the lake	**o lago** *oo lah·goo*
the mountain	**a montanha** *uh maun·tah·nyuh*
the nature preserve	**a reserva natural** *uh reh·zehr·vuh nuh·too·rahl*
the view point	**o miradouro** *oo mee·ruh·dau·roo*
the park	**o parque** *oo pahrk*
the path	**o caminho para peões [pedestres]** *oo kuh·mee·nyoo puh·ruh pee·oingz [peh·dehs·trehz]*
the peak	**o pico** *oo pee·koo*
the picnic area	**a área de piqueniques** *a ahr·ee·uh deh pee·keh·nee·kehz*
the pond	**a lagoa** *uh luh·gaw·uh*
the river	**o rio** *oo rree·oo*
the sea	**o mar** *oo mahr*
the valley	**o vale** *oo vahl*
Where's…?	**Onde é…?** *aund eh…*
the vineyard	**a vinha** *uh vee·nyuh*
the waterfall	**a cascata** *uh kuhz·kah·tuh*

Going Out

ESSENTIAL

What is there to do in the evenings?	**O que há para se fazer à noite?** *oo keh ah puh•ruh seh fuh•zehr ah noyt*
Do you have a program of events?	**Tem um programa dos espectáculos?** *teng oong proo•gruh•muh dooz ee•spehk•tah•koo•looz*
What's playing at the movies [cinema] tonight?	**O que há no cinema hoje à noite?** *oo kee ah noo see•neh•muh auzseh ah noyt*
Where's…?	**Onde é…?** *aund eh…*
the downtown area	**o centro** *oo sehn•troo*
the bar	**o bar** *oo bar*
the dance club	**a discoteca** *uh deez•koo•teh•kuh*
Is there a cover charge?	**É preciso pagar entrada [ingresso]?** *eh preh•see•zoo puh•gahr ehn•trah•duh [een•greh•soo]*

Carnaval is widely celebrated both in Portugal and Brazil.
A time of lavish celebration before Lent, **Carnaval** begins four
days before Ash Wednesday, and ends with the famous 'Fat Tuesday'
celebration. Look for parades on the streets and carnival balls (**bailes
carnavalescos**). The famed **Carnaval do Rio** sees the spectacularly
colorful competition between the various samba schools in a parade
through the streets of Rio de Janeiro.

Samba and bossa nova are the dance styles best known abroad, but
regional rhythms like **pagode**, **lambada**, **frevo**, **forró**, **maracatu**,
baião, **carimbó** and **bumba-meu boi**, with their mixture of African,
Indian, and European influences, are also very popular with locals and
tourists.

Entertainment

Can you recommend…?	**Pode recomendar-me…?**	*pawd reh•koo•mehn•dahr•meh…*
a concert	**um concerto**	*oong kaun•sehr•too*
a movie	**um filme**	*oong feel•meh*
an opera	**uma ópera**	*oo•muh aw•peh•ruh*
a play	**um teatro**	*oong tee•ah•troo*
When does it start/end?	**A que horas começa/acaba?**	*uh kee aw•ruhz koo•meh•suh/uh•kah•buh*
What's the dress code?	**O que é o código de vestido?**	*oo kee eh oo kaw•dee•goo deh vehs•tee•thoo*
I like…	**Gosto de…**	*gaws•too deh…*
classical music	**música clássica**	*moo•zee•kuh klah•see•kuh*
folk music	**música popular**	*moo•zee•kuh poo•poo•lahr*
jazz	**jazz**	*zsahz*

| pop music | **pop** *pawp* |
| rap | **rap** *rahp* |

A popular evening activity in Portugal is a visit to a **casa de fados** (house of blues), an intimate, late-night restaurant where your meal is accompanied by the melodies of the **fado**, the national folk song.

Local papers and weekly entertainment guides—such as **Sete** in Portugal and **Veja** in Brazil—will tell you what's on. Regional booklets (**vejinha**) are also useful in Brazil.

YOU MAY HEAR...

Desligue os seus telefones móveis [celulares], por favor. *dehz·lee·geh oohz sehooz tehl·fawnz maw·vayz [sehl·oo·lahrz] poor fuh·vaur*

Turn off your cell [mobile] phones, please.

Nightlife

What is there to do in the evenings?	**O que há para se fazer à noite?** *oo keh ah puh·ruh seh fuh·zehr ah noyt*
Can you recommend...?	**Pode recomendar-me...?** *pawd reh·koo·mehn·dahr·meh...*
a bar	**um bar** *oong bar*
a casino	**um casino** *oong kuh·see·noo*
a dance club	**uma discoteca** *oo·muh dee·skoo·teh·kuh*

a gay club	**um clube gay** *oong kloob gay*
a jazz club	**um clube de jazz** *oong kloob deh zsahz*
a club with Portuguese music?	**uma discoteca com música Portuguesa?** *oo•muh dee•skoo•teh•kuh kaum moo•zee•kuh poor•too•gehza*
Is there live music?	**Há música ao vivo?** *ah moo•zee•kuh ahoo vee•voo*
How do I get there?	**Como é que vou até lá?** *kau•moo eh keh vauoo uh•teh lah*
Is there a cover charge?	**É preciso pagar entrada [ingresso]?** *eh preh•see•zoo puh•gahr ehn•trah•duh [een•greh•soo]*
Let's go dancing.	**Vamos dançar.** *vuh•mooz duhn•sahr*
Is this area safe at night?	**Esta zona é segura à noite?** *eh•stuh zau•nuh eh seh•goo•ruh ah noyt?*

Portugal offers the usual range of nightclubs along the coast; most don't begin to get lively until around midnight.

Special Requirements

ESSENTIAL

I'm here on business.	**Estou aqui em negócios.** ee-_stawoo_ uh-_kee_ eng neh-_gaw_-see-oosz
Here's my business card.	**Tome o meu cartão.** _taw_-meh oo meeoo kuhr-_tohm_
Can I have your card?	**Posso ter o seu cartão?** _paw_-soo tehr oo sehoo kuhr-_tohm_
I have a meeting with...?	**Tenho um apontamento com...** _tay_-nyoo oong uh-paun-tuh-_mehn_-too kaum...
Where's...?	**Onde é...** _aund_ eh...
the business center	**o centro de negócios** oo _sehn_-troo deh neh-_gaw_-see-oosz
the convention hall	**o lugar de convenção** oo loo-_gahr_ deh kaun-vehn-_sohmz_
the meeting room	**o lugar de reunião** oo loo-_garh_ deh rree-oo-nee-_ohmz_

On Business

I'm here to attend...	**Estou aqui para participar...** ee-_stawoo_ uh-_kee_ puh-ruh puhr-tee-see-_pahr_...
a seminar	**num seminário** noong seh-mee-_nah_-ree-oo
a conference	**numa conferência** _noo_-muh kaun-feh-_rehn_-see-uh
a meeting	**numa reunião** _noo_-muh rree-oo-nee-_ohm_
My name is...	**Chamo-me... [Meu nome é...]** _shuh_-moo meh... [mehoo _naum_-ee eh...]

May I introduce my colleague…	**Posso apresentar o meu colega _m_ /a minha colega _f_…** <u>paw</u>·soo uh·preh·zehn·<u>tahr</u> oo mehoo koo·<u>leh</u>·guh/uh <u>mee</u>·nyuh koo·<u>leh</u>·guh…
I have a meeting/ an appointment with…	**Tenho uma reunião/um apontamento com…** <u>tay</u>·nyoo <u>oo</u>·muh rree·oo·nee·<u>ohm</u>/oong uh·paun·tuh·<u>mehn</u>·too kaum…
I'm sorry I'm late.	**Desculpe, estou atrasado _m_ /atrasada _f_.** dehs·<u>kool</u>·puh ee·<u>stawoo</u> uh·truh·<u>zah</u>·thoo/ uh·truh·<u>zah</u>·thuh
I need an interpreter.	**Preciso de um tradutor.** preh·<u>see</u>·zoo deh oong truh·doo·<u>taur</u>
You can reach me at the…Hotel.	**Pode encontrar-me no hotel…** <u>pawd</u>·eh eng·kaun·<u>trahr</u>·meh noo aw·<u>tehl</u>…
I'm here until…	**Estou aqui até…** ee·<u>stawoo</u> uh·<u>kee</u> uh·<u>teh</u>…
I need to…	**Preciso de…** preh·<u>see</u>·zoo deh…
make a call	**fazer um telefonema** fuh·<u>zehr</u> oong teh·leh·faw·<u>neh</u>·muh
make a photocopy	**fazer uma fotocópia** fuh·<u>zehr</u> <u>oo</u>·muh faw·taw·<u>kaw</u>·pee·uh
send an e-mail	**enviar um e-mail** eng·vee·<u>ahr</u> oong ee·<u>mehl</u>
send a fax	**enviar um fax** ehn·vee·<u>ahr</u> oong fahks

Business culture in Portugal respects age and position, and holds to strict rules of behavior. Never interrupt a business colleague during a presentation; hand gestures are considered rude and are not used to express feelings; appointments are mandatory and lateness unacceptable; eye contact is essential. Do not use high-pressure sales tactics, as aggressive behavior is often seen as offensive.

send a package (overnight)	**enviar um embrulho (de um dia para o outro)** *ehn·vee·ahr oong eng·broo·lyoo (deh oong dee·uh puh·ruh oo aw·troo)*
It was a pleasure to meet you.	**Muito prazer.** *mooee·too pruh·zehr*

For Communications, see page 52.

YOU MAY HEAR...

Você tem um apontamento?
vaw·seh teng oo uh·paun·tuh·mehn·too

Do you have an appointment?

Com quem? *kaum keng*

With whom?

Está numa reunião. *ee·stah noo·muh ree·oo·nee·ohm*

He/She is in a meeting.

Um momento, por favor. *oong moo·mehn·too poor fuh·vaur*

One moment, please.

Sente-se. *sehn·tuh·suh*

Have a seat.

Quer qualquer coisa para beber?
kehr kwahl·kehr coy·zuh puh·ruh beh·behr

Would you like something to drink?

Obrigado m /Obrigada f por vir.
aw·bree·gah·thoo/aw·bree·gah·thuh poor veer

Thank you for coming.

Traveling with Children

ESSENTIAL

Is there a discount for children?	**Há desconto para crianças?** *ah dehs·caun·too puh·ruh kree·uhn·suhs*
Can you recommend a babysitter?	**Pode recomendar-me uma babysitter [babá] qualificada?** *pawd reh·koo·mehn·dahr·meh oo·muh bay·bee·sit·tur [bah·buh] kwahl·ee·fee·kah·duh*
Do you have a child's seat?	**Pode trazer uma cadeirinha de criança?** *pawd truh·zehr oo·muh kuh·day·ree·nyuh deh kree·uhn·suh*
Where can I change the baby?	**Onde posso mudar o bebé [neném]?** *aund paw·soo moo·dahr oo beh·beh [neh·neh]*

Out & About

Can you recommend something for the kids?	**Pode recomendar-me algo próprio para crianças?** *pawd reh·koo·mehn·dahr·meh ahl·goo praw·pree·oo puh·ruh kree·uhn·suhs*
Where's…?	**Onde é…?** *aund eh…*
the amusement park	**o parque de diversões** *oo pahr·keh deh dee·vehr·sohmz*
the arcade	**o salão de jogos** *oo suh·lohm deh zsaw·gooz*
the kiddie [paddling] pool	**a piscina de bebés [nenéns]** *uh pee·see·nuh deh beh·behz [neh·nehnz]*
the park	**o parque** *oo pahrk*
the playground	**o parque de recreio [playground]** *oo pahrk deh reh·kray·oo [play·graund]*
the zoo	**o jardim zoológico** *oo zsuhr·deem zoo·law·zsee·koo*
Are kids allowed?	**São permitidas crianças?** *sohm pehr·mee·tee·thuhz kree·uhn·suhz*

Is it safe for kids?	**É seguro para as crianças?** *eh seh·goo·roo puh·ruh uhz kree·uhn·suhs*
Is it suitable for… year olds?	**Será bom para crianças com…anos?** *seh·rah bohng puh·ruh kree·uhn·suhz kaum…uh·nooz*

For Numbers, see page 173.

YOU MAY HEAR…

Que giro! *keh zsee·roo*	How cute!
O que é o nome dele/dela? *oo kee eh oo nau·meh dehl/deh·luh*	What's his/her name?
Quantos anos tem ele/ela? *kwuh·tooz uh·nooz teng ehl/eh·luh*	How old is he/she?

Baby Essentials

Do you have…?	**Tem…?** *teng…*
a baby bottle	**um biberom** *oong bee·brohng*
baby wipes	**os toalhetes de limpeza para o bebé [nenê]** *ooz too·ah·lyehtz deh leem·peh·zuh puh·ruh oo beh·beh [neh·neh]*

a car seat	**um assento de carro** *oong uh•sehn•too deh kah•r*
a children's menu/ portion	**uma ementa/dose [porção] de criança** *oo•muh ee•mehn•tuh/daw•zeh [poor•sohm] deh kree•uhn•suh*
a child's seat	**uma cadeirinha de criança** *oo•muh kuh•day•ree•nyuh deh kree•uhn•suh*
a crib	**uma cama de bebé [neném]** *oo•muh kuh•muh de beh•beh [neh•neh]*
diapers [nappies]	**as fraldas** *uhz frahl•duhz*
formula	**fórmula de bebé [neném]** *fawr•moo•luh deh beh•beh [neh•neh]*
a pacifier [dummy]	**uma chupeta** *oo•muh shoo•peh•tuh*
a playpen	**um parque para crianças** *oong pahr•kuh puh•ruh kree•uhn•suhz*
a stroller [pushchair]	**uma cadeira de bebé [neném]** *oo•muh kuh•day•ruh deh beh•beh [neh•neh]*
Can I breastfeed the baby here?	**Posso amamentar o bebé [neném] aqui?** *paw•soo uh•muh•mehn•tahr oo beh•beh [neh•neh] uh•kee*
Where can I change the baby?	**Onde posso mudar o bebé [neném]?** *aund paw•soo moo•thahr oo beh•beh [neh•neh]*

For Dining with Children, see page 68.

Babysitting

Can you recommend a reliable babsitter?	**Pode recomendar-me uma babysitter [babá] qualificada?** *pawd reh•koo•mehn•dahr•meh oo•mu bay•bee•sit•tur [bah•bah] kwah•lee•fee•kah•thuh*
What's the charge?	**Qual é o preço?** *kwahl eh oo preh•soo*
I'll be back by…	**Volto às…** *vawl•too ahz…*
I can be reached at…	**Pode-me encontrar…** *pawd•meh ng•kaun•trahr…*

For Time, see page 175.

Health & Emergency

Can you recommend a pediatrician? **Pode recomendar um pediatra?** *pawd reh·kau·mehn·dahr oong pee·dee·ah·truh*

My child is allergic to... **A minha criança é alérgico m /alérgica f a...** *uh mee·nyuh kree·uhn·suh eh uh·lehr·gee·koo/ uh·lehr·gee·kuh uh...*

My son/daughter is missing. **O meu filho/A minha filha desapareceu.** *oo mehoo fee·lyoo/uh mee·nyuh fee·lyuh deh·zuh·puh·ruh·seoo*

Have you seen a boy/ girl? **Viu um menino/uma menina?** *veeoo oong meh·nee·noo/oo·muh meh·nee·nuh*

For Health, see page 159.

Disabled Travelers

ESSENTIAL

Is there...? **Há...?** *ah...*

access for the disabled **acesso para deficientes físicos** *uh·seh·soo puh·ruh deh·fee·see·ehntz fee·see·kooz*

a wheelchair ramp **uma rampa de cadeira de rodas** *oo·muh ruhm·puh deh kuh·day·ruh deh raw·thuhz*

a handicapped- [disabled-] accessible toilet **uma casa de banho acessível para deficientes** *oo·muh kah·zuh deh buh·nyoo uh·seh·see·vehl puh·ruh deh·fee·see·ehntz*

I need... **Preciso de...** *preh·see·zoo deh...*

assistance **assistência** *uh·see·stehn·see·uh*

an elevator [lift] **um elevador** *oong eh·leh·vuh·daur*

a ground-floor room **um quarto no primeiro andar** *oong kwahr·too noo pree·may·roo uhn·dahr*

Asking for Assistance

I'm disabled.	**Sou deficiente.** *sawoo deh·fee·see·ehnt*
I'm deaf.	**Sou surdo m /Sou surda f.** *sawoo soor·doo/sawoo soor·duh*
I'm visually/hearing impaired.	**Vejo/Ouço mal.** *vay·zsoo/ow·soo mahl*
I'm unable to walk far/ use the stairs.	**Não posso caminhar muito/usar as escadas.** *nohm paw·soo kuh·mee·nyahr mween·tuh/oo·zahr uhz ee·skah·thuhz*
Please speak louder.	**Por favor, fale mais alto.** *poor fuh·vaur fah·leh mey·ez ahl·too*
Can I bring my wheelchair?	**Posso trazer a minha cadeira de rodas?** *paw·soo truh·zehr uh mee·nyuh kuh·day·ruh deh raw·duhz*
Are guide dogs permitted?	**Os cães de guia são permitidos?** *ooz kengs de gee·uh sohm pehr·mee·tee·dooz*
Can you help me?	**Pode ajudar-me?** *pawd uh·zsoo·dahr·meh*
Please open/hold the door.	**Por favor abra/segure a porta.** *poor fuh·vaur ah·bruh/seh·goo·reh uh pawr·tuh*

In an Emergency

Emergencies

ESSENTIAL

Help!	**Socorro!** soo-_kau_-rroo
Go away!	**Vá-se embora!** _vah_-seh ehng-_baw_-ruh
Call the police!	**Chame a polícia!** _shuh_-meh uh poo-_lee_-see-uh
Stop thief!	**Pára ladrão!** _pah_-ruh luh-_drohm_
Get a doctor!	**Chame um médico!** _shuh_-meh oong _meh_-dee-koo
Fire!	**Fogo!** _fau_-goo
I'm lost.	**Estou perdido m /perdida f.** ee-_stawoo_ pehr-_dee_-thoo/pehr-_dee_-thuh
Can you help me?	**Pode ajudar-me?** pawd uh-zsoo-_dahr_-meh

In Portugal, dial **112** for the police, ambulance or fire brigade. In Brazil, dial **190** for the police, **192** for the ambulance, and **193** for the fire brigade.

YOU MAY HEAR...

Preencha este formulário. | Fill out this form.
pree-_eng_-sheh eh-stuh _fawr_-muh-lah-reeoo

A sua identificação, por favor. uh _soo_-uh | Your identification,
ee-dehnt-tee-fee-kuh-_sohm_ por fuh-_vaur_ | please.

Quando/Onde é que foi? _kwuhn_-doo/ | When/Where did it
aund eh keh foy | happen?

Como é ele/ela? _kau_-moo eh ehleh/ehluh | What does he/she look like?

Police

ESSENTIAL

Call the police!	**Chame a polícia!** _shuh•meh uh poo•lee•see•uh_
Where's the police station?	**Onde é a esquadra [delegacia] da polícia?** _aund eh uh ee•skwahr•duh [deh•leh•guh•see•uh] thuh poo•lee•see•uh_
There has been an accident/attack.	**Houve um acidente/ataque.** _auoo•veh oong uh•see•dehnt/uh•tah•keh_
My son/daughter is missing.	**O meu filho/A minha filha desapareceu.** _oo mehoo fee•lyoo/uh mee•nyuh fee•lyuh deh•zuh•puh•ruh•seoo_
I need...	**Preciso de...** _preh•see•zoo deh..._
an interpreter	**um tradutor** _oong truh•doo•taur_
I need...	**Preciso de...** _preh•see•zoo deh..._
to contact my lawyer	**contactar o meu advogado** _kaun•tuhk•tahr oo mehoo uhd•voo•gah•thoo_
to make a phone call	**fazer um telefonema** _fuh•zehr oong teh•leh•foo•neh•muh_
I'm innocent.	**Sou inocente.** _sawoo ee•naw•sehnt_

Crime & Lost Property

I want to report...	**Quero reportar...** _keh•roo reh•paur•tahr..._
a mugging	**um assalto** _oong uh•sahl•too_
a rape	**uma violação [um estupro]** _oo•muh vee•au•luh•sohm [oong ee•stoo•proo]_
a theft	**um roubo** _oong rau•boo_
I've been robbed.	**Fui roubado m /roubada f.** _fooee raw•bah•thoo/ raw•bah•thuh_

I've been mugged.	**Fui assaltado** *m* /**assaltada** *f*. *fooee uh•sahl•tah•thoo/uh•sahl•tah•duh*
I've lost my…	**Perdi…** *pehr•thee…*
My…has/have been stolen.	**Roubaram-me…** *raw•bah•rohm•meh…*
backpack	**a mochila** *uh moo•sheeh•luh*
bicycle	**a bicicleta** *uh bee•see•kleh•tuh*
camera	**a máquina fotográfica** *uh mah•kee•nuh faw•too•grah•fee•kuh*
(hire) car	**o carro (alugado)** *oo kah•rroo (uh•loo•gah•doo)*
computer	**o computador** *oo kaum•poo•tuh•daur*
credit card	**os cartão de crédito** *ooz kuhr•tohm deh kreh•dee•too*
jewelry	**as jóias** *uhz zsoy•uhz*
money	**o dinheiro** *oo dee•nyay•roo*
passport	**o passaporte** *oo pah•suh•pawrt*
purse [handbag]	**a carteira** *uh kuhr•tay•truh*
traveler's checks [cheques]	**os cheques de viagem.** *ooz shehkz deh vee•ah•zseng*
wallet	**a carteira (de documentos)** *uh kuhr•tay•ruh (deh doo•koo•mehn•tooz)*

I need a police report.	**Preciso de um documento da policia.**
	preh-<u>see</u>-zoo deh oong thoo-koo-<u>mehn</u>-too duh
	poo-<u>lee</u>-see-uh
Where is the British/	**Onde fica a embaixada Britânica/Americana/**
American/Irish	**Irlandesa?** aund fee-kuh uh ehm-beye-shah-duh
embassy?	bree-tuhn-nee-kuh/uh-meh-ree-kuh-nuh/
	eer-luhn-deh-zuh

Health

ESSENTIAL

I'm sick [ill].	**Estou doente.** ee-<u>stawoo</u> doo-<u>ehnt</u>
I need an English-	**Preciso de um médico que fale inglês.**
speaking doctor.	preh-<u>see</u>-zoo deh oong <u>meh</u>-dee-koo keh <u>fah</u>-leh
	eeng-<u>lehz</u>
It hurts here.	**Dói-me aqui.** <u>doy</u>-meh uh-<u>kee</u>
I have a stomachache.	**Tenho uma dor de estômago.** <u>teh</u>-nyoo <u>oo</u>-muh
	daur deh ee-<u>stau</u>-muh-goo

Finding a Doctor

Can you recommend	**Pode recomendar um médico/dentista?** pawd
a doctor/dentist?	reh-koo-mehn-<u>dahr</u> oong <u>meh</u>-dee-koo/dehn-<u>teeh</u>-stuh
Could the doctor come	**O médico podia vir cá ver-me [aqui me ver]?** oo
to see me here?	<u>meh</u>-dee-koo poo-<u>thee</u>-uh veer kah <u>vehr</u>-meh [uh-<u>kee</u>
	meh vehr]
I need an English-	**Preciso de um médico que fale inglês.**
speaking doctor.	preh-<u>see</u>-zoo deh oong <u>meh</u>-dee-koo keh
	<u>fah</u>-leh eeng-<u>lehz</u>

What are the office hours?	**A que horas é que há consulta?** *uh kee aw·ruhz eh keh ah kaun·sool·tuh*
I'd like to make an appointment...	**Queria marcar uma consulta...** *keh·ree·uh muhr·kahr oo·muh kaun·sool·tuh...*
for today	**para hoje** *puh·ruh auyzseh*
for tomorrow	**para amanhã** *puh·ruh uh·muh·nyuh*
as soon as possible	**o mais cedo possível** *oo meyez seh·thoo poo·see·vel*
It's urgent.	**É urgente.** *eh oor·zsehnt*

Symptoms

I'm...	**Estou...** *ee·stawoo...*
bleeding	**a sangrar [sangrando]** *uh suhn·grahr [suhn·gruhn·doo]*
constipated	**constipado m /constipada f** *kaun·stee·pah·thoo/kaun·stee·pah·thuh*
dizzy	**com a cabeça à roda** *kaum uh kuh·beh·suh ah raw·thuh*
I'm nauseous.	**Estou enjoado m /enjoada f.** *ee·stawoo eng·zsoo·ah·thoo/eng·zsoo·ah·thuh*
I'm vomiting.	**Estou a vomitar.** *ee·stawoo uh voo·mee·tahr*
It hurts here.	**Dói-me aqui.** *doy·meh uh·kee*
I have...	**Tenho...** *teh·nyoo...*
an allergic reaction	**uma reacção alérgica** *oo·muh rree·ah·sohm uh·lehr·gee·kuh*
chest pain	**dor de peito** *daur deh pay·too*
diarrhea	**diarreia** *dee·uh·rray·uh*
an earache	**dor de ouvidos** *daur deh aw·vee·thooz*
a fever	**uma febre** *oo·muh feh·breh*
pain	**dor** *daur*

a rash	**uma erupção cutânea** <u>oo</u>·muh eer·oop·<u>sohm</u> koo·<u>tuh</u>·nee·uh
a sprain	**uma distensão muscular** <u>oo</u>·muh dees·tehn·<u>sohm</u> <u>moos</u>·koo·lahr
some swelling	**algum inchaço** <u>ahl</u>·goong een·<u>shah</u>·soo
a stomachache	**dor de estômago** daur deh ee·<u>stau</u>·muh·goo
I have sunstroke.	**Apanhei uma insolação.** uh·puh·<u>nyay</u> <u>oo</u>·muh een·soo·luh·<u>sohm</u>
I've been sick [ill] for…days.	**Há…dias que me sinto doente.** ah…<u>dee</u>·uhz keh meh <u>seen</u>·too doo·<u>ehnt</u>

For Numbers, see page 173.

Conditions

I'm…	**Sou…** sawoo…
anemic	**anémico** m /**anémica** f uh·<u>neh</u>·mee·koo/ uh·<u>neh</u>·mee·kuh
asthmatic	**asmático** m /**asmática** f uhz·<u>mah</u>·tee·koo/ uhz·<u>mah</u>·tee·kuh
diabetic	**diabético** m /**diabética** f dee·uh·<u>beh</u>·tee·koo/ dee·uh·<u>beh</u>·tee·kuh
epileptic	**epiléptico** eh·pee·leh·tee·koo

I'm allergic to antibiotics/penicillin. **Sou alérgico m /alérgica f a antibióticos penicilina.** *sawoo uh·lehr·gee·koo/ uh·lehr·gee·kuh uh uhn·tee·bee·aw·tee·kuhz/ peh·neh·seh·lee·nuh*

I have arthritis. **Tenho artrite.** *teh·nyoo uh·treet*

I have a heart condition. **Tenho um problema de coração.** *teh·nyoo oong proo·bleh·muh deh koo·ruh·sohm*

I have high/low blood pressure. **Tenho a pressão arterial alta/baixa.** *teh·nyoo uh preh·sohm uhr·teh·ree·ahl ahl·tuh/beye·shuh*

I'm on... **Estou em...** *ee·stawoo eng...*

YOU MAY HEAR...

Qual é o problema? *kwahl eh oo proo·bleh·muh* — What's the problem?

Onde é que lhe dói? *aund eh keh lyeh doy* — Where does it hurt?

Dói-lhe aqui? *doy·lyeh uh·kee* — Does it hurt here?

Toma medicamentos? *taw·muh meh·dee·kuh·mehn·tooz* — Are you on medication?

É alérgico m /alérgica f a algo? *eh uh·lehr·zee·koo/uh·lehr·zee·kuh uh ahl·goo* — Are you allergic to anything?

Abra a boca. *ah·bruh uh bau·kuh* — Open your mouth.

Respire fundo. *rehs·pee·reh foon·doo* — Breathe deeply.

Tussa, por favor. *too·suh, poor fuh·vaur* — Cough, please.

Quero que vá para o hospital. *keh·roo keh vah puh·ruh oo aws·pee·tahl* — I want you to go to the hospital.

Treatment

Do I need medicine?	**Preciso de algum medicamento?** preh•see•zoo deh ahl•goong meh•dee•kuh•mehn•too
Can you prescribe a generic drug [unbranded medication]?	**Pode prescrever um medicamento genérico** pawd prehz•kreh•vehr oong meh•dee•kuh•mehn•too geh•neh•ree•koo
Where can I get it?	**Onde posso obtê-lo?** aund paw•soo au•bteh•loo

For What to Take, see page 166.

Hospital

Please notify my family.	**Por favor informe a minha família.** poor fuh•_vaur_ eeng•_fawr_•meh uh _mee_•nyuh fuh•_mee_•lyuh
I'm in pain.	**Estou com dores.** ee•_stawoo_ kaun daur•ehz
I need a doctor/nurse.	**Necessito um médico/uma enfermeira.** neh•seh•_see_•too oong _meh_•dee•koo/_oo_•muh een•fehr•_may_•ruh
When are visiting hours?	**Quais são as horas de visitas?** kweyez sohm uhz _aw_•ruhz deh vee•_zee_•tuhz
I'm visiting…	**Estou a visitar…** ee•_stawoo_ uh vee•see•_tahr_…

Dentist

I've broken a tooth/ lost a filling.	**Parti um dente./Perdi um chumbo.** pehr•thee oong dehnt/pehr•_thee_ oong _shoom_•boo
I have a toothache.	**Tenho dor de dentes.** _teh_•nyoo daur deh dehntz
Can you fix this denture?	**Pode consertar esta dentadura?** pawd kaun•sehr•_tahr_ eh•stuh dehn•tuh•_doo_•ruh

Gynecologist

I have menstrual cramps/a vaginal infection.	**Tenho dores de períodos menstruais/ uma infecção na vagina.** _teh_·nyoo daurz duh pehr·ree·_oo_·thooz mehn·stroo·_eyez_/_oo_·muh eeng·feh·_sohm_ nuh vuh·_zsee_·nuh
I missed my period.	**Faltou-me o meu período.** _fahl_·_tawoo_·meh oo meeoo peh·ree·_oo_·thoo
I'm on the pill.	**Estou a tomar [tomando] a pílula.** ee·_stawoo_ uh too·_mar_ [too·_muhn_·doo] uh _pee_·loo·luh
I'm (not) pregnant.	**(Não) Estou grávida.** (nohm) ee·_stawoo_ _grah_·vee·thuh
I haven't had my period for…months.	**Já não tenho o meu período há…meses.** zsah nohm _teh_·nyoo oo mehoo peh·ree·_oo_·thoo ah.. _meh_·zehz

Optician

I've lost…	**Perdi…** pehr·_thee_…
one of my contact lenses	**uma das minhas lentes de contacto** _oo_·muh duhz _mee_·nyuhz _lehn_·tehz deh kaun·_tahk_·too
my glasses	**os meus óculos** ooz mehooz _aw_·koo·looz
a lens	**uma lente** _oo_·muh lehnt

Payment & Insurance

How much?	**Quanto é?** _kwuhn_·too eh
Can I pay by credit card?	**Posso pagar com cartão de crédito?** _paw_·soo puh·_gahr_ kaum oo kuhr·_tohm_ deh _kreh_·dee·too
I have insurance.	**Tenho seguro.** _teh_·nyoo seh·_goo_·roo
Can you give me a receipt for my health insurance?	**Pode dar-me [Podia me dar] um recibo para o meu seguro de saúde?** pawd _dar_·meh [poo·_dee_·uh. meh dar] oong reh·_see_·boo _puh_·ruh oo mehoo seh·_goo_·roo deh suh·_oo_·theh

ESSENTIAL

Where's the pharmacy [chemist]?	**Onde fica a farmácia?** *aund fee•kuh uh fuhr•mah•see•uh*
What time does the pharmacy open/close?	**A que horas é que a farmácia abre/fecha?** *uh keh aw•ruhz eh keh uh fuhr•mah•see•uh ah•breh/feh•shuh*
What would you recommend for...?	**O que é que me recomenda para...?** *oo keh eh keh meh reh•koo•mehn•duh puh•ruh...*
How much should I take?	**Quanto é que devo tomar?** *kwuhn•too eh keh deh•voo too•mahr*
Can you fill [make up] this prescription for me?	**Pode aviar-me esta receita?** *pawd uh•vee•ahr•meh eh•stuh reh•say•tuh*
I'm allergic to...	**Sou alérgico m /alérgica f a...** *sawoo uh•lehr•zsee•koo/uh•lehr•zsee•kuh ah...*

Pharmacies are easily recognized by their sign: a green or red cross, usually lit up. You'll find the address of all-night pharmacies (**farmácia de serviço**) displayed in all pharmacy windows. In Portugal, pharmacies sell pharmaceutical products, and sometimes a small supply of cosmetics as well—also available in a **perfumaria**. Household items and toiletries can be bought from a **drogaria** or **mercearia**. In the pharmacies in Brazil, you can normally find medicines, perfume, cosmetics and household goods. Travelers who use prescription medicine should bring enough with them to cover their stay.

What to Take

How much should I take?	**Quanto é que devo tomar?** _kwuhn·too eh keh deh·voo too·mahr_
How often should I take it?	**Quantas vezes é que devo tomar?** _kwuhn·tuhz veh·zehz eh keh deh·voo too·mahr_
Is it suitable for children?	**É próprio para crianças?** _eh praw·pree·oo puh·ru kree·uhn·suhs_
I'm taking…	**Estou a tomar…** _ee·stawoo uh too·mahr…_

YOU MAY SEE…

UMA VEZ/TRÊS VEZES POR DIA	once/three times a day
COMPRIMIDO(S)	tablet(s)
GOTA	drop
COLHER(ES) DE CHÁ	teaspoon(s)
ANTES DAS/DEPOIS DAS/COM AS REFEIÇÕES	before/after/with meals
COM O ESTÔMAGO VAZIO	on an empty stomach
INGIRA INTEIRO	swallow whole
PODE CAUSAR SONOLÊNCIA	may cause drowsiness
PARA USO EXTERNO	for external use only

Are there side effects?	**Há efeitos colaterais?** *ah ee·fay·tooz kaw·luh·tehr·eyez*	
I'd like some medicine for...	**Queria um remédio para...** *keh·ree·uh oohn ruh·meh·dee·oo puh·ruh...*	
a cold	**uma constipação [um resfriado]** *oo·muh kaun·stee·puh·sohm [oong rehz·free·ah·do]*	
a cough	**a tosse** *uh taw·seh*	
diarrhea	**a diarreia** *uh dee·uh·rray·uh*	
a headache	**uma dor de cabeça** *oo·muh daur deh kuh·beh·suh*	
insect bites	**as picadas de insecto** *uhz pee·kah·duhz deh eeng·sehk·too*	
motion sickness	**o enjoo** *oo ehn·zsau·oo*	
a sore throat	**a dor de garganta** *uh daur deh guhr·guhn·tuh*	
sunburn	**uma queimadura de sol** *oo·muh kay·muh·doo·ruh deh sawl*	
a toothache	**uma dor de dentes** *oo·muh daur deh dehnts*	
an upset stomach	**uma indisposição gástrica** *oo·muh een·dees·poo·zee·sohm gahz·tree·kuh*	

Basic Supplies

I'd like...	**Queria...** *keh·ree·uh...*	
acetaminophen [paracetamol]	**paracetamol** *puh·ruh·seh·tuh·mawl*	
antiseptic cream	**uma pomada antiséptica** *oo·muh poo·mah·duh uhn·tee·sehp·tee·kuh*	
aspirin	**uma aspirina** *oo·muh uhz·pee·ree·nuh*	
bandages	**umas ligaduras [ataduras]** *oo·muhz lee·guh·doo·ruhz [uh·tuh·doo·ruhz]*	
a comb	**um pente** *oong pehnt*	
condoms	**uns preservativos** *oongz preh·sehr·vuh·tee·vooz*	

contact lens solution	**um líquido de lente de contacto** *oong lee·kee·thoo deh lehnt deh kaun·tahk·too*
deodorant	**um desodorizante** *oong dehz·aw·doo·ree·zuhnt*
a hairbrush	**uma escova de cabelo** *oo·muh ees·kau·vuh deh kuh·beh·loo*
I'd like...	**Queria...** *keh·ree·uh...*
hair spray	**laca [laquê] para o cabelo** *lah·kuh [lah·keh] puh·ruh oo kuh·beh·loo*
ibuprofen	**ibuprofeno** *ee·boo·praw·feh·noo*
insect repellent	**um repelente para insectos** *oong reh·peh·lehnt puh·ruh een·sehk·tooz*
a nail file	**uma lima** *oo·muh lee·muh*
a (disposable) razor	**uma gilete (descartável)** *oo·muh zsee·leht (dush·kuhr·tah·vehl)*
razor blades	**umas lâminas de barbear** *oo·muhz luh·mee·nuhz deh buhr·bee·ahr*
sanitary napkins [towels]	**uns pensos [absorventes] higiénicos** *oongz pehn·sooz [uhb·sawr·vehntz] ee·zseh·nee·kooz*
shampoo/ conditioner	**um shampoo [xampu]/amaciador [condicionador] para cabelo** *oong shuhm·poo [shuhm·poo] uh·muh·see·uh·daur [kaun·dee·see·oo·nuh·daur] puh·ruh kuh·beh·lo*
soap	**um sabonete** *oong suh·boo·neht*
sunscreen	**um protector solar** *oong praw·teh·taur soo·lahr*
tampons	**uns tampões higiénicos** *oongz tuhm·poingz ee·zseh·nee·kooz*
tissues	**uns lenços de papel** *oongz lehn·sooz deh puh·pehl*
toilet paper	**papel higiénico** *puh·pehl ee·zseh·nee·koo*
toothpaste	**uma pasta de dentes** *oo·muh pah·stuh deh dehntz*

For Baby Essentials, see page 151.

The Basics

Grammar

In Portuguese, there are three ways to say 'you' (taking different verb forms):
In Portugal, **tu** is used when talking to a relative your age or younger, a close
friend, a child and between young people; in Brazil, **tu** is hardly ever used. **Tu**
refers to just one person at a time, and it takes the second person singular form
of the verb.

In Portugal, **você(s)** is used in more formal situations, between people who
don't know each other well and as a sign of respect for family members, anyone
older than you, more educated than you or in business. In most parts of Brazil,
você is predominantly used when talking to anyone, regardless of age or class,
even in cases when **tu** would be used in Portugal. **Você(s)** takes either the third
person singular or the third person plural of the verb depending on whether
you're referring to one person (**você**) or more than one person (**vocês**).

The most formal way of saying 'you' is **o(s) senhor(es)** to a man (men) and
a(s) senhora(s) to a woman (women). This is the case in both Portugal and
Brazil. **O(s) senhor(es)** and **a(s) senhora(s)** take either the third person
singular of the verb or the third person plural depending on whether you're
referring to one person (**o senhor/a senhora**) or more than one person (**os
senhores/as senhoras**).

Regular Verbs

Here are three of the main categories of regular verbs in the present tense:

	-ar falar (to speak)	-er comer (to eat)	-ir cobrir (to cover
eu	falo	como	cubro
tu	falas	comes	cobres
ele/ela/você	fala	come	cobre
nós	falamos	comemos	cobrimos
vós	falais	comeis	cobris
eles/elas/vocês	falam	comem	cobrem

Irregular Verbs

In Portuguese there are two main verbs meaning 'to be', both of which are irregular.

Ser indicates a permanent state:

Sou inglês. I'm English.
É portuguesa. She is Portuguese.

Estar indicates movement or a temporary state:

Está doente. He is sick [ill].
Estou a passear [passeando]. I am walking.

Nouns & Articles

Nouns in Portuguese are either masculine or feminine. Masculine nouns usually end in **-o** and feminine nouns in **-a**. Normally nouns that end in a vowel become plural by adding an **-s**.

Articles must agree with the noun to which they refer in gender and number.

Indefinite: **um carro** (a car); **uns carros** (some cars); **uma casa** (a house); **umas** casas (some houses)

Definite: **o carro** (the cars); **os carros** (some cars); **a casa** (the house); **as casas** (the houses)

Word Order

In Portuguese, the conjugated verb comes after the subject.
Maria fala inglês. Maria speaks English.
To ask a question, reverse the order of the subject and verb, change your
intonation or use key question words such as **quando** (when).
Quando abre o museu? When does the museum open?
Literally translates to: 'When opens the museum?'
É portuguesa? Is she Portuguese?
Literally: She is Portuguese? This is a statement that becomes a question by
raising the pitch of the last syllable of the sentence.

Negation

To form a negative sentence, add **não** (not) before the verb.
Fumamos. We smoke.
Não fumamos. We don't smoke.

Imperatives

Imperative sentences, commands, are formed by adding the appropriate
ending to the stem of the verb.
Fale! Speak!
Abra a janela, por favor. Open the window, please.

Comparative & Superlative

The comparative is usually formed by adding **mais** (more) or **menos** (less)
before the adjective or noun. The superlative is formed by adding the
appropriate definite article (**o/os**, **a/as**) and **mais** (the most) or **menos** (the
least).

alto	**mais alto**	**o mais alto**
tall	taller	tallest
caro	**menos caro**	**o menos caro**
expensive	less expensive	least expensive

Possessive Pronouns

Pronouns serve as substitutes for specific nouns and must agree with the noun in gender and number.

meu *m* /**minha** *f*	mine
teu *m* /**tua** *f*	yours
seu *m* /**sua** *f*	yours (formal)
nosso *m* /**nossa** *f*	ours
vosso *m* /**vossa** *f*	yours (plural)

Example: **Esse assento é meu.** That seat is mine.

Adjectives

Adjectives describe nouns and must agree with the noun in gender and number. In Portuguese, adjectives usually come after the noun. Masculine adjectives usually end in **-o**, feminine adjectives in **-a**. If the masculine form ends in **-e** (**intellegente**) or with a consonant (**fácil**), the feminine form is generally the same.

O filho/A filha é amável. Your son/daughter is nice.

O mar/A flor azul. The blue ocean/flower.

Adverbs & Adverbial Expressions

Adverbs are used to describe verbs. Some adverbs are formed by adding **-mente** to the singular feminine form of the adjective.

Example: **sincera + mente = sinceramente**

The following are some common adverbial time expressions:

agora	now
ainda não	not yet
ainda	still
nunca	never
sempre	always

Numbers

ESSENTIAL

0	**zero** _zeh_·roo
1	**um** _m_ **/uma** _f_ oong/_oo_·muh
2	**dois** _m_ **/duas** _f_ doyz/_thoo_·uhz
3	**três** trehz
4	**quatro** _kwah_·troo
5	**cinco** _seeng_·koo
6	**seis** sayz
7	**sete** seht
8	**oito** _oy_·too
9	**nove** nawv
10	**dez** dehz
11	**onze** aunz
12	**doze** dauz
13	**treze** trehz
14	**catorze** kuh·_taurz_
15	**quinze** keengz
16	**dezasseis [dezesseis]** dehz·eh·_sayz_
17	**dezassete [dezessete]** dehz·eh·_seht_
18	**dezoito** dehz·_oy_·too
19	**dezanove [dezenove]** deh·zuh·_nawv_
20	**vinte** veent
21	**vinte e um** _m_ **/uma** _f_ veent ee oong/_oo_·muh
22	**vinte e dois** _m_ **/duas** _f_ veent ee doyz/_thoo_·uhz
30	**trinta** _treeng_·tuh
31	**trinta e um** _m_ **/uma** _f_ _treeng_·tuh ee oong/_oo_·muh
40	**quarenta** kwuh·_rehn_·tuh
50	**cinquenta** seeng·_kwehn_·tuh

173

60	**sessenta** seh·_sehn_·tuh
70	**setenta** seh·_tehn_·tuh
80	**oitenta** oy·_tehn_·tuh
90	**noventa** noo·_vehn_·tuh
100	**cem** sehn
101	**cento e um** m /**uma** f _sehn_·too ee oong/_oo_·muh
200	**duzentos** m /**duzentas** f doo·_zehn_·tooz/doo·_zehn_·tuhz
500	**quinhentos** m /**quinhentas** f kee·_nyehn_·tooz/kee·_nyehn_·tuhz
1,000	**mil** meel
10,000	**dez mil** dehz meel
1,000,000	**um milhão** oong mee·_lyohm_

Ordinal Numbers

first	**o primeiro** m /**a primeira** f oo pree·_may_·roo/uh pree·_may_·ruh
second	**o segundo** m /**a segunda** f oo seh·_goon_·doo/uh seh·_goon_·duh
third	**o terceiro** m /**a terceira** f oo tehr·_say_·roo/uh tehr·_say_·ruh
fourth	**o quarto** m /**a quarta** f oo _kwahr_·too/uh _kwahr_·tuh
fifth	**o quinto** m /**a quinta** f oo _keen_·too/uh _keen_·tuh
once	**uma vez** _oo_·muh vehz
twice	**duas vezes** _thoo_·uhz _veh_·zehz
three times	**três vezes** trehz _veh_·zehz

Portuguese uses a comma for a decimal point and a period [full stop] or space for thousands, e.g. 4,95; 4.575.000 or 4 575 000.

Time

ESSENTIAL

What time is it?	**As horas, por favor?** *uhz aw•ruhz poor fuh•vaur*
It's noon [mid-day].	**É meio-dia.** *eh may•oo dee•uh*
At midnight.	**À meia-noite.** *ah may•uh noyt*
From nine o'clock to five o'clock.	**Das nove às cinco horas.** *duhz nawv ahz seeng•koo aw•ruhz*
Twenty [after] past four.	**Quatro e vinte.** *kwah•troo ee veent*
A quarter to nine.	**Um quarto para as nove.** *oong kwahr•too puh•ruh uhz nawv*
5:30 a.m./p.m.	**Cinco e meia de manhã/da tarde.** *seeng•koo ee may•uh deh muh•nyuh/duh tahrd*

In Portugal, digital time is on the 24-hour clock, but time is not referred to in that way. The Portuguese would not say it's '13:00,' in speech but rather they would express the hour along with the time of day, i.e. 'one in the afternoon' (**uma hora da tarde**).

Days

ESSENTIAL

Monday	**segunda-feira** seh·<u>goon</u>·duh <u>fay</u>·ruh
Tuesday	**terça-feira** <u>tehr</u>·suh <u>fay</u>·ruh
Wednesday	**quarta-feira** <u>kwahr</u>·tuh <u>fay</u>·ruh
Thursday	**quinta-feira** <u>keen</u>·tuh <u>fay</u>·ruh
Friday	**sexta-feira** <u>say</u>·stuh <u>fay</u>·ruh
Saturday	**sábado** <u>sah</u>·buh·thoo
Sunday	**domingo** doo·<u>meeng</u>·goo

Portuguese calendars go from Monday to Sunday. When giving dates, the Portuguese give the day first, then the month, then the year (e.g. 1 May 2009 or 1/5/2009).

Dates

yesterday	**ontem** <u>awn</u>·teng
today	**hoje** auzseh
tomorrow	**amanhã** uh·muh·<u>nuh</u>
day	**o dia** oo <u>dee</u>·uh
week	**a semana** uh seh·<u>muh</u>·nuh
month	**o mês** oo mehz
year	**o ano** oo <u>uh</u>·noo

Months

January	**Janeiro** zher·<u>nay</u>·roo
February	**Fevereiro** feh·<u>vray</u>·roo
March	**Março** <u>mahr</u>·soo
April	**Abril** uh·<u>breel</u>

May	**Maio** _meye_•oo
June	**Junho** _zsoo_•nyoo
July	**Julho** _zsoo_•lyoo
August	**Agosto** uh•_gaus_•too
September	**Setembro** seh•_tehm_•broo
October	**Outubro** aw•_too_•broo
November	**Novembro** noo•_vehm_•broo
December	**Dezembro** deh•_zehm_•broo

Seasons

the spring	**a primavera** uh pree•muh•_veh_•ruh
the summer	**o verão** oo vrohm
the fall [autumn]	**o outono** oo aw•_too_•noo
the winter	**o inverno** oo eeng•_verr_•noo

The dates of **Carnaval** are based on the dates of Lent and Easter, and therefore change every year. **Carnaval** starts on the Saturday before Ash Wednesday and lasts until Ash Wednesday.

Holidays

Some major national holidays in Portugal and Brazil are:

January 1	New Year's Day	Port.	Braz.
January 6	Epiphany	Port.	Braz.
April 11	Tiradentes Day		Braz.
April 25	Freedom Day	Port.	
May 1	May Day	Port.	Braz.
June 10	Camões Day	Port.	
August 15	Assumption Day	Port.	Braz.
September 7	Independence Day		Braz.

October 1	Our Lady of Aparecida Day		Braz.
October 5	Republic Day	Port.	
November 1	All Saints' Day	Port.	Braz.
November 15	Proclamation Day		Braz.
December 1	Restoration Day	Port.	
December 8	Immaculate Conception Day	Port.	Braz.
December 25	Christmas Day	Port.	Braz.

Conversion Tables

When you know	Multiply by	To find
ounces	28.3	grams
pounds	0.45	kilograms
inches	2.54	centimeters
feet	0.3	meters
miles	1.61	kilometers
square inches	6.45 sq.	centimeters
square feet	0.09 sq.	meters
square miles	2.59 sq.	kilometers
pints (U.S./Brit)	0.47/0.56	liters
gallons (U.S./Brit)	3.8/4.5	liters
Fahrenheit	5/9, after 32	Centigrade
Centigrade	9/5, then +32	Fahrenheit

Kilometers to Miles Conversions

1 km – 0.62 mi	**20 km** – 12.4 mi
5 km – 3.10 mi	**50 km** – 31.0 mi
10 km – 6.20 mi	**100 km** – 61.0 mi

Measurement

1 gram	**grama**	= 0.035 oz.
1 kilogram (kg)	**quilo**	= 2.2 lb
1 liter (l)	**litro**	= 1.06 U.S/0.88 Brit. quarts
1 centimeter (cm)	**centimetro**	= 0.4 inch
1 meter (m)	**metro**	= 3.28 ft.
1 kilometer (km)	**quilómetro**	= 0.62 mile

Temperature

-40° C – -40° F	**-1° C** – 30° F	**20° C** – 68° F
-30° C – -22° F	**0° C** – 32° F	**25° C** – 77° F
-20° C – -4° F	**5° C** – 41° F	**30° C** – 86° F
-10° C – 14° F	**10° C** – 50° F	**35° C** – 95° F
-5° C – 23° F	**15° C** – 59° F	

Oven Temperature

100° C – 212° F	**149° C** – 300° F	**204° C** – 400° F
121° C – 250° F	**177° C** – 350° F	**260° C** – 500° F

Dictionary

A

abbey a abadia
able capaz
about àcerca de
above acima
abroad no estrangeiro
abscess o abcesso
accept aceitar
access o acesso
accident o acidente
accidentally sem querer
accommodation o alojamento
accompany acompanhar
accountant o contabilista
  [contador]
activity a actividade
across do outro lado
adaptor o adaptador
address o endereço, a morada
admission charge o preço de
  entrada
adult o adulto
aerobics aeróbica
after depois
afternoon tarde

aftershave a loção para depois da
  barba [a loção após barba]
after-sun lotion a loção para
  depois do sol
age a idade
ago há
agree concordar
air conditioning o ar condicionado
air mattress o colchão pneumático
  [o colchão de ar]
air pump a máquina pneumática
  [a bomba de ar]
airline a linha aérea
airmail a via aérea
airport o aeroporto
aisle seat o lugar na coxia
  [o lugar de corredor]
alarm clock o despertador
alcoholic drink a bebida alcoólica
all tudo
allergic alérgico
allergy a alergia
allow permitir
almost quase
alone sózinho

| **adj** adjective | **BE** British English | **prep** preposition |
| **adv** adverb | **n** noun | **v** verb |

already já
also também
alter modificar
alternate route a rota alternada [o caminho alternativo]
aluminum foil o papel de alumínio
always sempre
ambassador o embaixador
ambulance a ambulância
American o americano, a americana
anesthetic a anestesia [o anestéstico]
and e
announcement anúncio
another outro, outra
answer atender [responder]
antibiotic o antibiótico
antifreeze o anticongelante
antique a antiguidade
antiseptic cream a pomada antiséptica
any algum
anyone else mais alguém
anyone alguém
anything alguma coisa
apartment o apartamento
apologize pedir desculpa
apology a desculpa
appointment o apontamento [o encontro]
approximately aproximadamente

archery o tiro ao arco
architect o arquitecto, a arquitect
architecture a arquitectura
area a área
area code o indicativo [código]
around (the corner) ao virar da esquina
arrange arranjar
arrivals (airport) as chegadas
arrive chegar
art a arte
art gallery a galeria de arte
artificial sweetener o adoçante
artist o/a artista
ashtray o cinzeiro
ask pedir
asleep adormecido, adormecida
aspirin a aspirina
at least pelo menos
athletics atletismo
attack o ataque
attendant o empregado, a empregada
attractive atraente
aunt a tia
Australia a Austrália
Australian o australiano, a australiana
authentic autêntico
authenticity autenticidade
automatic (car) o carro de

mudanças automáticas

automatic teller machine (ATM)
o multibanco

avalanche a avalanche

away longe

awful horrível

B

baby o bebé [neném];
~**sitter** baby-sitter [a ama];
~**wipes** os toalhetes de limpeza
para o bebé [neném]

baby bottle o biberom
[a mamadeira]

back as costas

bachache a dor de costas

backpack a mochila

bacon toucinho

bad mau, má

bakery a padaria

balcony a varanda

ball a bola

ballet o ballet [o balê]

band (musical) a banda musical

bandage a ligadura [a atadura]

bank o banco

bar o bar

barber o barbeiro

baseball basebol

basement a cave

basin a bacia

basket o cesto

basketball basquetebol

bath o banho

bathe tomar banho

bathroom a casa de banho
[o banheiro]

battery a pilha; ~ **(car, computer)**
a bateria

battle site o campo de batalha

be v ser; ~ **(temporary
state)** estar; ~ **(location)** ficar

beach a praia

beard a barba

beautiful bonito, bonita

because porque; ~ **of** por causa de

bed a cama; ~ **and breakfast**
quarto e pequeno-almoço
[pernoite e café da manhã]

bedding a roupa de cama

bedroom o quarto (de dormir)

bee a abelha

beer a cerveja

before antes de

begin v começar

beginner o/a principiante

beginning o começo

beige beige [bege]

belong pertencer

belt o cinto

best melhor

better melhor

between entre
bib a babete [o babador]
bicycle a bicicleta
big grande
bigger o/a maior
bikini o bikini [o biquini]
binoculars os binóculos
bird o pássaro
bishop o bispo
bite (insect) a picada (de insecto)
bitter azedo
bizarre estranho
black preto
blanket o cobertor
bleach a lixívia [alvejante]
blouse a blusa
blow-dry o secador
blue azul
blueberry o mirtilo
board embarcar
boarding (plane) embarque
boarding pass cartão de embarque
boat o barco
boiled cozido
book n o livro
book v reservar
book of tickets a caderneta de bilhetes
bookstore a livraria
boots as botas
border a fronteira

boring aborrecido
botanical garden o jardim botânico
bottle a garrafa; ~ **opener** o abre-garrafas [o abridor de garrafas]
bowl a malga
box office a bilheteira
boxing o boxe
boy o rapaz
boyfriend o namorado
bra o sutiã
bracelet a pulseira
brake n o travão [o freio]
brass o latão
Brazil o Brasil
Brazilian brasileiro
bread o pão
break v partir [quebrar]
breakdown avariar [quebrar]
break-in o assalto
breakfast o pequeno-almoço [o café da manhã]
breathe v respirar
bridge a ponte
briefcase a pasta
briefs as calcinhas
brilliant brilhante
bring v trazer
Britain a Grã-Bretanha
British britânico

brochure o folheto
bronze o bronze
brother o irmão
brown o castanho
brush a escova
bucket (pail) o balde
build v construir
building o edifício
built construído
burger o hambúrguer
burglary o roubo
burnt queimado
bus o autocarro; ~ **(long-distance)**
a camioneta; ~ **station** a estação
de autocarros; ~ **stop** a paragem
[a parada] de autocarro
business class (em) business;
~ **a trip** viagem de negócios
business card o cartão
busy ocupado
but mas
butcher shop o talho [o açougue]
butter a manteiga
button o botão
buy v comprar
bye adeus [adeus]

C

cabin a cabina [o camarote]
cable car o funicular; o teleférico
café o café

cake o bolo
calendar o calendário
call v chamar
camcorder a câmara de vídeo
camera a máquina fotográfica;
~ **case** o estojo para a máquina;
~ **store** a loja de artigos
fotográficos
camp v acampar
camping campismo [camping];
~ **equipment** o material de
campismo [camping]
campsite o parque de campismo
[camping]
can n a lata; ~ **opener** o abre-
latas [o abridor de latas]
Canadá o Canadá
Canadian canadiano [canadense]
canal o canal
cancel v cancelar
cancer (disease) o cancro [o
câncer]
candle a vela
candy os rebuçados [as balas]
canoe a canoa
canoeing fazer canoagem
canyon o desfiladeiro
car o carro; ~ **hire [BE]** aluguer
[aluguel] de carros; ~ **park [BE]** o
parque de estacionamento;
~ **rental** aluguer [aluguel] de

carros
carafe o jarro
card o cartão; **ATM ~** o cartão
multibanco; **credit ~** o cartão
de crédito; **debit ~** o cartão de
débito; **phone ~** o cartão de
chamadas
cards as cartas
carpet o tapete
carry transportar
carry-on levar
carton o pacote
cash o dinheiro
cash v cobrar
casino o casino
castle o castelo
cat o gato [a gata]
catch v **(bus)** apanhar o autocarro
[o ônibus]
cathedral a catedral
cause v causar
cave a caverna
CD o CD
CD-player o leitor de CDs
[o tocador de discos compactos]
cell phone o telemóvel
celcius celsius
cemetery o cemitério
cent o cêntimo
certificate o certificado
chair a cadeira

change n **(coins)** trocado;
~ v **(bus)** mudar (de autocarro);
~ v **(clothes)** trocar (de roupa);
~ v **(money)** trocar dinheiro;
~ v **(reservation)** mudar a
reserva
changing rooms os vestiários
channel (sea) o canal
chapel a capela
charcoal o carvão
charge a tarifa
cheap barato
cheaper mais barato
check (bill) a conta; **put it on the**
~ ponha na conta
check v verificar
checkbook o livro [talão] de
cheques
check-in desk o balcão de registo
[de registro]
check out v **(hotel)** pagar a conta
checking account a conta corrente
checkout (supermarket) a caixa
cheers à sua saúde
cheese o queijo
chemical toilet a fossa séptica
chemist [BE] a farmácia
chickenpox a varicela
child o menino [a criança]
child's seat a cadeirinha de criança;
~ **(in car)** a cadeira de criança

chips [BE] as batatas fritas
church a igreja
cigarette o cigarro
cigars os charutos
cinema o cinema
class a classe
clean *adj* limpo [limpa]
clean *v* limpar
cleaner (person) o empregado da limpeza; **~ (product)** o produto de limpeza
cliff a falésia
cling film [BE] o papel aderente
clock o relógio
close (near) perto
close *v* fechar
clothes a roupa; **~ dryer** a máquina de secar [o centrifugador]
clothing store a loja de artigos de vestuário
cloudy nublado
clubs (golf) os tacos de golfe
coast a costa
coat o casaco [comprido]
cockroach a barata
coffee o café
coin a moeda
cold frio; **~ (illness)** a constipação [o resfriado]
colleague o colega
college o colégio

color a cor
comb o pente
comedy a comédia
comforter o edredão
commission a comissão
compartment (train) o compartimento
compass o compasso
complain reclamar
complaint a reclamação
computer o computador
conditioner (hair) o amaciador [o condicionador] para o cabelo
condom o preservativo
conductor (orchestra) o maestro
conference a conferência
confirm *v* confirmar
confirmation a confirmação
connect ligar [conectar]
connection (flight) ligação
conscious consciente
constipation a prisão de ventre
consulate o consulado
contact *v* contactar
contact lens as lentes de contacto
contain *v* conter
contageous contagioso
contraceptive o contraceptivo
convenient conveniente
cook o cozinheiro, a cozinheira
cook *v* cozinhar

cool (temperature) fresco
copper o cobre
corkscrew o saca-rolhas
corn o milho
corner a esquina
correct correcto
cost o custo
cot a cama de bebé [neném], o berço
cotton o algodão
cough *n* a tosse; ~ *v* tossir
country (nation) o país
countryside o campo
couple (pair) o par
course (meal) o prato
cousin o primo [a prima]
crash *n* **(car)** o desastre [o acidente]
credit card o cartão de crédito; ~ **number** o número do cartão de crédito
cross *v* **(road)** atravessar
crowded com muita gente
cruise o cruzeiro
crystal o cristal
cup a chávena
cupboard o armário
currency a moeda
currency exchange (office) loja de câmbio
customs a alfândega; ~ **declaration** declaração da

alfândega
cut *n* o corte; ~ *v* cortar
cycling [BE] o ciclismo

D

daily diariamente
damage avariado
damp húmido
dance *n* a dança; ~ *v* dançar; ~ **club** o clube de dansa
dangerous perigoso
dark escuro
daughter filha
dawn a madrugada
day o dia
dead morto; ~ **(battery)** descarregada
deaf surdo
debit card (Port) o cartão de débito
deck chair a cadeira de encosto
declare *v* declarar
decline o declínio
deduct *v* **(money)** deduzir
deep profundo
degrees (temperature) os graus
delay o atraso
delete (computer) apagar
delicatessen a charcutaria
delicious delicioso
deliver *v* entregar

denim a ganga [brim]
dental floss o fio dental
dentist o dentista
deodorant o desodorizante
 [o desodorante]
depart v (train, bus) partida
department store o grande
 armazém [loja de departamentos]
departure (train) a partida
depend depende
deposit n o depósito
deposit v depositar
destination o destino
detergent detergente
diabetes os diabetes
diabetic o diabético
diamonds os diamantes
diaper a fralda
diarrhea a diarreia
dictionary o dicionário
diesel o gasóleo [diesel]
difficult difícil
digital digital
dining room a sala de jantar
dinner o jantar
direct adj directo
direct v indicar
direction a direcção
directory (telephone) a lista
 telefónica
dirty sujo, suja

disabled (person) o/a deficiente
disconnect (computer) desligar
 [desconectar]
discount o desconto
dish (meal) o prato
dishes a louça
dishwashing liquid o detergente
 para a louça
display case a vitrina
disposable (camera) máquina
 descartável
dive v mergulhar
divorced divorciado
doctor o médico
dog o cão
doll a boneca
dollar (U.S.) o dólar
domestic (flight) domestico
door a porta
double bed a cama de casal
double room o quarto duplo
down abaixo
downstairs em baixo
downtown o centro da cidade
dozen dúzia
dress n (clothing) vestido
drink n bebida
drinking water água potável
drive v conduzir
driver condutor
driver's license a carta de

condução [carteira de motorista]
drugstore a farmácia
drunk o bêbado
dry cleaner a lavandaria
[lavanderia] de limpeza a seco
during durante
dusty poeirento
duty (tax) dever
duty-free goods a mercadoria
isenta de taxas
duty-free shopping as compras
duty-free

E

ear o ouvido
ear drops gotas para os ouvidos
earlier mais cedo
early cedo
earrings os brincos
east leste
easy fácil
eat comer
economy class a classe económica
electricity a electricidade
elevator o elevador
e-mail *n* o email; *v* enviar emails
e-mail address morada de email
embassy a embaixada
emerald a esmeralda
emergency a emergência;
~ **exit** a saída de emergência

empty *adj* vazio [vazia]
enamel (jewelry) esmalte
end *v* terminar
engine o motor
England a Inglaterra
English inglês
enjoy *v* apreciar
enough bastante [suficiente]
enter entrar
entertainment entretenimento
envelope o envelope
equipment (sports) o
equipamento (desportivo)
erase *v* apagar
error o erro
escalator a escada rolante
essential essencial
e-ticket o bilhete electrónico
EU (European Union) a UE
(União Europeia)
euro o euro
Europe a Europa
except excepto
excess o excesso
exchange *v* trocar
exchange rate a taxa de câmbio
excursion a excursão
excuse me (apology) desculpe-
me; **(to get attention)** desculpe
exhausted *adj* exausto [exausta]
exhibition a exposição

exit a saída
expensive caro
expiration date a data de validade
extremely extremamente
eye o olho

F

face a cara
facial a limpeza de pele
family a família
famous famoso
fan (electric) a ventoinha [o ventilador]
far longe
fare o bilhete
farm a quinta
fast depressa
faster mais rápido
fast food as refeições rápidas
fat n a gordura; adj gordo
fat-free sem gordura
father o pai
faucet a torneira
favorite o preferido, a preferida
fax n o fax
fax v enviar fax
fear o medo
feed v alimentar
female a mulher
ferry o ferry
few poucos

fever a febre
field (sports) o campo
fill out v (form) preencher
film (camera) o filme
fine (penalty) a multa
fire n o fogo
fire alarm o alarme de incêndio
fire department [brigade] os bombeiros
fire escape a saída de incêndio
fire extinguisher o extintor de incêndio
first o primeiro
first class a primeira classe
first-aid kit o estojo de primeiros socorros
fit (clothes) servir
fitting room o gabinete de provas
fix v arranjar
flag a bandeira
flash (photography) o flash
flashlight a lanterna
flat (tire) o furo
flight o vôo
floor (level) o andar
flower a flor
fly (insect) a mosca
fly v voar
food a comida
football [BE] o futebol
forecast a previsão

foreign o estrangeiro; **~ currency** as divisas estrangeiras
forest a floresta
forget v esquecer
fork (utensil) o garfo; **~ (in road)** a bifurcação
form o impresso
formula (baby) a papa
fortunately felizmente
fountain a fonte
free (available) livre; **~ (no charge)** grátis
frequently muitas vezes, frequentemente
fresh fresco
friend o amigo, a amiga
full cheio
furniture a mobília

G

gallon o galão
game o jogo
garage a garagem [a oficina]
garbage bag o saco para o lixo
garden o jardim
gardener o jardineiro
gasoline a gasolina
gate (airport) a porta
gay club o clube gay
genuine autêntico, autêntica
get out v sair

gift a oferta
girl a menina
girlfriend a namorada
give v dar
give way (on the road) [BE] dar prioridade
glass (drinking) o copo
glass (material) o vidro
glove a luva
go ir
golf o golfe
good bom [boa]; **~ morning** bom dia; **~night** boa noite
goodbye adeus
gram o grama
grandparent o avô, a avó
grape a uva
gray o cinzento
green o verde
grocery store a mercearia
ground (camping) o terreno
group o grupo
guarantee a garantia
guide (person) o/a guia
guidebook o guia

H

hair o cabelo; **~ gel** o gel para o cabelo; **~brush** a escova de cabelo; **~dryer** o secador de cabelo; **~spray** a laca para o cabelo

haircut o corte de cabelo

hairdresser (ladies/men)
o cabeleireiro (senhoras/homens)

half metade

hammer o martelo

hand a mão

hand cream o creme para as mãos

hand luggage [BE] a bagagem
de mão

handbag [BE] a mala de mão

handicapped o/a deficiente

handicapped accessible acessível
a deficientes

hangover a ressaca

happy feliz

hat o chapéu

have v ter

head a cabeça

health a saúde

hear v ouvir

hearing aid o aparelho auditivo

heater o aquecedor

heating [BE] aquecedor

heavy pesado

height a altura

hello olá

help n a ajuda

help v ajudar

here aqui

high a altura

high tide a maré alta

highway a auto-estrada

hike (walk) o passeio a pé

hiking fazer longas caminhadas
a pé

hill a colina

hire v [BE] alugar

hire car [BE] o carro de aluguer
[o carro de aluguel]

hitchhike v pedir boleia [carona]

hold v (contain) conter

holiday o feriado

holiday [BE] as férias

home a casa

horse o cavalo

horseracing a corrida de cavalos

hospital o hospital

hostel a pensão

hot (temperature) quente;
(spicy) picante

hot spring a nascente de água
quente

hot water a água quente

hotel o hotel

hour a hora

house a casa

household goods os artigos para
a casa

how (question) como

how much (question) quanto

hurt adj o ferido, a ferida

husband o marido

I

ice o gelo
ice cream o gelado, o sorvete;
  ~ parlor a gelataria [a sorveteria];
  ~ cone o cone de gelado [sorvete]
ice hockey o hóquei no gelo
icy *adj* gelado, gelada
identification a identificação
ill *adj* o/a doente
illness a doença
in (place) no; **(time)** em
indoor dentro de casa; **~ pool** a
  piscina coberta
inexpensive barato
inflammation a inflamação
informal (dress) (o vestido)
  informal
information a informação
innocent o/a inocente
insect o insecto; **~ bite** a picada
  de insecto; **~ repellent** o
  repelente de insectos
inside dentro de
insomnia a insónia
instant coffee o café instantâneo
instant message a mensagem
  instantânea
insulin a insulina
insurance o seguro;

  ~ card a apólice de seguro
interesting interessante
international internacional
internet cafe o internet café
internet service o serviço de
  internet
interpreter o/a intérprete
intersection o cruzamento
introduce *v* introduzir
invite *v* convidar
Ireland a Irlanda
Irish irlandês
iron *v* passar a ferro
island a ilha

J

jam doce
jar o frasco
jeans as calças de ganga
jellyfish a alforreca [a água-viva]
jewelry as jóias
joke a piada
judge o juiz, a juiza
jumper cables os cabos da bateria

K

key a chave
key card o cartão da porta
kiddie pool a piscina de bebés
  [nenens]
kilo(gram) o quilo(grama)

kilometer o quilómetro
kiosk o quiosque
kiss beijar
kitchen a cozinha
knee o joelho

L

lace a renda
ladder a escada
lake o lago
large grande
last o último
late (time) tarde;
  (delayed) atrasado
later mais tarde
launderette [BE] a lavandaria
  [a lavanderia]
laundromat a lavandaria
  [a lavanderia]
laundry service o serviço de
  lavandaria [lavanderia]
lawyer o advogado, a advogada
learn v aprender
leather o cabedal [o couro]
leave v partir
left a esquerda
left-luggage office [BE] o
  depósito de bagagem
lens a objectiva
less menos
lesson a lição

letter a carta
library a biblioteca
life a vida
lifeboat o barco salva-vidas
lifeguard o banheiro/salva-vidas
life jacket o colete salva-vidas
lift [BE] o elevador
light (shade) claro; **(weight)** leve
light n a luz; v ascender
lightbulb a lâmpada (eléctrica)
lighter o isqueiro
lightning o relâmpago
line (waiting) a fila (de espera)
line (subway) a linha
linen o linho
lip o lábio
liquor store a loja de bebidas
  alcoólicas
liter o litro
little pequeno, pequena
live v viver
local regional
lock n a fechadura
locked adj fechado, fechada
locker o cacifo com fecho
log on v autenticar
log off v sair
long comprido; **(time)** muito
long-sighted [BE] visto de longe
look v ver
look for procurar

lose *v* perder
lost *adj* perdido
lost-and-found os perdidos e achados
lotion a loção
louder mais alto
love (a person) amar; **(a thing)** gostar de
luggage a bagagem
luggage cart [trolley] o carrinho
luggage locker o cacifo de bagagem
luggage ticket o talão de bagagem
lumpy (mattress) aos altos e baixos
lunch o almoço
lung o pulmão

M

magazine a revista
magnificent magnífico, magnífica
mail o correio
mailbox a caixa do correio
main course o prato principal
make up a prescription [BE] receitar
male o homem
man o homem
manager o/a gerente
manicure a manicure
manual (gears) (a caixa de velocidades) manual map o mapa
market o mercado
married casado
mass (church service) a missa
massage a massagem
matches (fire) os fósforos
material o material
mattress o colchão
maybe talvez
meal a refeição
mean *v* significar
measure *v* medir
measurement o tamanho
meat a carne
medicine o remédio
medium (size) médio; **(cooked)** meio-passado
meet *v* encontrar(-se)
mend *v* consertar
menu o menu
message a mensagem
metal o metal
meter (taxi) o taxímetro
meter (parking) o parquímetro
microwave (oven) o microondas
midday [BE] o meio-dia
migraine a enxaqueca
mileage a quilometragem
minibar o mini-bar [o frigobar]
minute o minuto
mirror o espelho

miss v perder
missing em falta
mistake o engano
misunderstanding o mal-entendido
mobile phone [BE] o telemóvel
mobile home a casa ambulante
modern moderno, moderna
money o dinheiro
monument o monumento
moped a lambreta
more mais
mosquito o mosquito
mother a mãe
motion sickness o enjoo
motor o motor
motorbike a motocicleta
motorboat o barco a motor
motorway [BE] a auto-estrada
mountain a montanha; ~ **bike** a bicicleta de montanha
moustache o bigode
mouth a boca
move v mudar(-se)
movie o filme
movie theater o cinema
much muito
mug (drinking) a caneca
mugging o assalto
mumps a papeira [a caxumba]
museum o museu

music a música

N

nail (body) a unha; ~ **polish** o verniz [o esmalte] de unhas
name o nome
napkin o guardanapo
nappy [BE] a fralda
narrow estreito
national nacional
nationality a nacionalidade
nature preserve a reserva natural
nausea a náusea
near perto
nearest mais próximo
necessary necessário
neck (body) o pescoço; (clothing) a gola
necklace o colar
needle a agulha
neighbor o vizinho, a vizinha
nephew o sobrinho
never nunca
new novo, nova
newspaper o jornal
newsstand [newsagent] o quiosque [a banca] de jornais
next próximo, próxima
next to ao lado de
niece a sobrinha
night a noite

nightclub o nightclub
no não
no one ninguém
noisy barulhento
non-alcoholic não-alcoólico, não-alcoólica
non-smoking adj não-fumadores [não-fumantes]
none nenhum, nenhuma
normal normal
north o norte
note a nota
note [BE] a nota
notebook o caderno
nothing nada
now agora
number (telephone) o número de telefone
number plate (car) [BE] a placa de matrícula
nurse o enfermeiro, a enfermeira

O

observatory o observatório
occupied ocupado, ocupada
off-licence [BE] a loja de vinhos
office o escritório
often muitas vezes
oil o óleo
okay O.K.
old o velho, a velha

old-fashioned antigo, antiga
one um, uma
one-way ticket o bilhete de ida
open v abrir
open adj aberto, aberta
opening hours as horas de funcionamento
opera a ópera
operation a operação
opposite o oposto
optician o oculista
orange (fruit) a laranja; (color) cor-de-laranja
orchestra a orquestra
order v encomendar
outdoor ao ar livre; ~ **pool** a piscina ao ar livre
outside fora de
over sobre
overdone adj cozido demais
overnight só uma noite

P

pacifier a chupeta
pack v fazer as malas
package o embrulho [o pacote]
paddling pool [BE] a piscina de bebés [nenens]
padlock o cadeado [o aloquete]
pain a dor
paint v pintar

painter o pintor, a pintora
painting o quadro
pajamas o pijama
palace o palácio
pants as calças
pantyhose os collants
paper o papel
paper napkin o guardanapo de papel
park o parque
park *v* estacionar
parking o estacionamento; ~ **lot** o parque de estacionamento; ~ **meter** o parquímetro; ~ **space** o lugar de estacionamento
partner o companheiro, a companheira
part a peça
party a festa
pass *n* o passe
pass *v* passar
passenger o passageiro, a passageira
passport o passaporte
pastry shop a pastelaria [a confeitaria]
patch *v* remendar
path o caminho
pay *v* pagar
pay phone o telefone público
peak (mountain) o pico

pearl a pérola
pedestrian crossing a passadeira [a passagem de pedestres]
pedicure a pedicure
pen a caneta
pencil o lápis
penicillin a penicilina
per por: ~ **day** por dia; ~ **hour** por hora; ~ **night** por noite; ~ **week** por semana
performance a sessão
perfume o perfume
perhaps talvez
period período
permit a permissão; *v* permitir
petrol [BE] a gasolina; ~ **station [BE]** a bomba de gasolina
pharmacy a farmácia
phone o telefone; ~ **call** o telefonema; ~ **card** o credifone [o cartão telefónico]
photo a fotografia
photocopier a fotocopiadora
photographer o fotógrafo, a fotógrafa
photography a fotografia
pick up *v* ir buscar; (collect) levantar
picnic o piquenique; ~ **area** a área para piqueniques
piece a peça

pill (birth control) a pílula
pillow a almofada
personal identification number (PIN) o PIN
pink cor-de-rosa
piste [BE] a pista; **~ map [BE]** o mapa de pistas
pizzeria a pizzaria
place o lugar; **(a bet)** apostar
plane o avião
plant a planta
plastic wrap o papel aderente
plate o prato
platform [BE] a linha [plataforma]
platinum a platina
play v jogar; **(instrument)** tocar
please se faz favor [por favor]
plug (electric) a ficha [a tomada] (eléctrica)
plunger o desentupidor
pocket o bolso
poison o veneno
police a polícia; **~ report** o documento da polícia; **~ station** a esquadra [a delegacia] da polícia
pond a lagoa
pool a piscina
pop music a música pop
popcorn as pipocas
popular popular
port (harbor) o porto

Portugal Portugal
Portuguese português
post [BE] o correio; **~ office** os correios
postbox [BE] a caixa do correio
postcard o postal, [o cartão postal]
poster o cartaz
pottery a cerâmica
pound (British sterling) a libra (esterlina)
pregnant a grávida
prescribe prescrever
prescription a receita
press v **(clothing)** passar a ferro [engomar]
pretty bonito, bonita
print v imprimir [impressar]
problem o problema
prohibit proibido
pronounce v pronunciar
public o público
pull v puxar
pump a bomba; **(gas)** a bomba c[gasolina
puncture [BE] o furo

Q

quality a qualidade
question a pergunta
queue [BE] n a fila
quiet sossegado, sossegada

R

race (cars, horses) a corrida;
~ **track** o hipódromo
racket (sports) a raquete
railway station [BE] a estação
de caminhos de ferro [a estação
ferrovíaria]
rain v chover
raincoat a gabardine
rape a violação [o estupro]
rare (unusual) raro, rara;
(steak) mal-passado,
mal-passada
razor a navalha; ~ **blade** a lâmina
de barbear
read v ler
ready pronto, pronta
real (genuine) de lei
receipt a factura [o recibo]
reception (desk) a recepção
receptionist o/a recepcionista
recommend v recomendar
red vermelho, vermelha
refrigerator o frigorífico [a
geladeira]
region a região
regular (gas/petrol) normal
rent v alugar
rental car o carro alugado
repair v arranjar
repeat v repetir

reservation a marcação
reserve v reservar
restaurant o restaurante
restroom a casa de banho
[o banheiro]
return v **(come back)** voltar;
(give back) devolver
right (correct) certo; ~ **of way**
prioridade
ring o anel
river o rio
road a estrada
robbed roubado, roubada
robbery o roubo
romantic romântico
room o quarto; ~ **service** o serviço
de quarto
round redondo, redonda
round-trip de ida e volta
route o caminho
rowboat o barco a remos
rubbish [BE] o lixo; ~ **bin [BE]**
o caixote do lixo
ruins as ruínas

S

sad triste
safe n o cofre; adj seguro
safety a segurança
sales tax IVA
same o mesmo, a mesma

sand a areia
sandals as sandálias
sanitary napkin o penso higiénico [a toalha higiénica]
saucepan o tacho [a caçarola]
sauna o sauna
save guardar
savings account a conta de poupança
scanner o scanner
scarf o lenço de pescoço
schedule o horário
school a escola
scissors a tesoura
sea o mar
seat o lugar
see ver
self-service self-service [auto-serviço]
sell v vender
send v mandar
senior citizen o reformado, a reformada [o idoso, a idosa]
separated separado, separada
serious sério, séria
service charge a taxa de serviço
set menu a ementa turística
sex o sexo
sexually transmitted disease (STD) Doença Sexualmente Transmissível (DST)
shallow pouco fundo, funda
shampoo o shampoo [o xampu]
sharp afiado, afiada
shaving cream o creme da barba
sheet o lençol
ship o navio
shirt a camisa
shoe o sapato; ~ **store** a sapataria
shopping compras; ~ **area** a zona comercial; ~ **centre [BE]** o centro comercial; ~ **mall** o centro comercial
short curto
shorts os calções
short sighted [BE] de vistas curtas
show n o espectáculo; v mostrar
shower o chuveiro
sick doente
side (of road) o lado; ~**effect** o efeito secundário; ~ **order** à parte; ~ **street** transversal
sidewalk o passeio
sightseeing tour o circuito turístico
sign o sinal
silk a seda
silver a prata
single (not married) solteiro; ~ **room** o quarto individual

sink o lava-louças [a pia]

sister a irmã

sit v sentar(-se)

size o número/tamanho

skin a pele

skirt a saia

skis os skis [esquis]

sleep dormir

sleeping bag o saco-cama [osaco de dormir]

sleeper car [BE] couchette [vagão-leitos]

slice a fatia

slippers os chinelos [as pantufas]

slope (ski) a rampa

slow lento, lenta

slower mais devagar

slowly devagar

small pequeno, pequena

small change troco

smoke v fumar

smoking (area) zona de fumadores [fumantes]

snack bar o snack bar [a lanchonete], a cafetaria

sneakers as sapatilhas [os ténis]

snorkel mergulho sem garrafa [snorkel]

snow a neve; v nevar

snowboard a prancha de snowboard

soap o sabonete

soccer o futebol

sock a peúga, meia [meia curta]

soft drink (soda) o refresco

sold out a lotação esgotada

someone alguém

something alguma coisa

sometimes às vezes

son o filho

sore throat a dor de garganta

sorry desculpe

south sul

souvenir a lembrança

spa o spa

speak falar

speed limit o limite de velocidade

speed v ir com excesso de velocidade

spell soletrar

spend gastar

spine a espinha

sponge a esponja

sport o desporto [o esporte]

sporting goods store a loja de artigos de desporto [esportivos]

spring a primavera

square o quadrado

stadium o estádio

stairs as escadas

stamp o selo

start começar

starter [BE] hors-d'oeuvre, o aperitivo
station a estação
station wagon a carrinha [minivan]
statue a estátua
stay permanecer
steal roubar
steep íngreme
sting o espeto
stolen roubado
stomach o estômago
stop n (bus, tram) a paragem [parada]
stop v parar
store guide a planta da loja
storey [BE] o prédio
straight ahead sempre em frente
stream o ribeiro
street a estrada
stroller a cadeira de bebé [neném]
student o/a estudante
study v estudar
subway o metro; ~ **station** a estação de metro
suit o fato [o terno]
suitcase a mala de viagem
sun o sol
sun block o protector solar
sunbathe tomar banho de sol
sunburn a queimadura de sol

sunglasses os óculos de sol
super (fuel) super
supermarket o supermercado
surfboard a prancha de surf
sweatshirt a sweatshirt [blusa de moleton]
sweet (taste) doce
sweets [BE] os rebuçados [as balas]
swim v nadar
swimsuit o fato [maiô] de banho
symbol o símbolo
synagogue a sinagoga

T

table a mesa
tablet (medicine) o comprimido
take v (carry) levar; (medicine) tomar; (time) demorar
take away [BE] para levar
tampons os tampões higiénicos
taste v provar
taxi o táxi; ~ **stand** a praça [o ponto] de táxis
team a equipa [o time]
teaspoon a colher de chá
telephone o telefone
tennis o ténis
tent a tenda; ~ **peg** a cavilha; ~ **pole** a estaca
terminal (airport) o terminal
text v (send a message) escrever

uma mensagem; *n*
(message) texto
thank you obrigado
that esse, essa
theater teatro
theft roubo
there ali
thief ladrão
thigh coxa
thirsty com sede
this este, esta
throat a garganta
ticket o bilhete; ~ **machine** a
   máquina de venda de bilhetes;
   ~ **office** a bilheteira [a bilheteria]
tie (clothing) a gravata
time as horas
timetable [BE] o horário
tire o pneu
tired cansado, cansada
tissue o lenço de papel
today hoje
toe o dedo do pé
together juntos
toilet a casa de banho
toilet paper o papel higiénico
tomorrow amanhã
tongue a língua
tonight hoje à noite; **for ~** para
   hoje à noite
too (much) demasiado;

(also) também
tooth o dente
toothbrush a escova de dentes
toothpaste a pasta de dentes
tour a visita
tourist o/a turista
towel a toalha
town a cidade; ~ **hall** a câmara
   municipal; ~ **map** o mapa de
   cidade
toy o brinquedo
toy store o armazém [a loja] de
   brinquedos
track o trilho
traffic o trânsito; ~ **jam** o
   engarrafamento; ~ **circle** a
   rotunda; ~ **light** o semáforo
trail o caminho; ~ **map** o mapa
train o comboio [o trem];
   ~ **station** a estação de caminho
   de ferro [a estação ferroviária]
transfer (plane, train) o
   transbordo
translate *v* traduzir
trash o lixo; ~ **can** a lixeira
travel *v* viajar;
   ~ **agency** a agência de viagens
traveler's check o cheque de
   viagens
tree a árvore
trip a excursão

trolley o carrinho
trousers [BE] as calças
T-shirt a T-Shirt [a camiseta]
TV a televisão [a TV]
type o tipo
tyre [BE] o pneu

U

ugly feio, feia
umbrella (rain) o guarda-chuva
unbranded medication [BE]
 o medicamento genérico
uncle o tio
unconscious perder os sentidos
underground [BE] o
 metropolitano; ~ station [BE] a
 estação de motropolitano
underpants as cuecas
understand compreende
United Kingdom o Reino Unido
United States os Estados Unidos
university a universidade
unleaded (gas) sem chumbo
unlimited (mileage) sem limite
 (de quilometragem)
unlock v abrir
upper superior
upstairs em cima
use v usar
use n uso
useful útil

username o nome de utilizador
utensil o utensílio

V

vacancy o quarto vago
vacation as férias
vaccination a vacinação
vacuum cleaner o aspirador
vagina a vagina
valid válido
valley o vale
valuable de valor
value o valor
VAT (sales tax) IVA
vegetarian vegetariano
vehicle o veículo; ~ registration
 os documentos do carro
veterinarian o veterinário
 a veterinária
view point [BE] o miradouro
village a aldeia
vineyard a vinha
visa o visto
visit n a visita
visit v visitar
visitor center o centro de
 acolhimento
visually impaired os invisuais
vitamin a vitamina
volleyball o voleibol
vomit vomitar

W

wait esperar

waiting room a sala de espera

waiter o empregado [o garcon]

waitress a empregada [a garçonete]

wake-up call a chamada para despertar

walk *v* dar um passeio

walking passear

walking route o itinerário a pé

wall a parede

wallet a carteira (de documentos)

warm *adj* morno, morna; *v* aquecer

wash *v* lavar

washing machine a máquina de lavar

watch *n* o relógio; *v* ver

water a água

water skis os skis aquáticos [os esquis-aquáticos]

weather o tempo; ~ **forecast** a previsão do tempo

wedding o casamento; ~ **ring** a aliança

week a semana

weekend o fim-de-semana

weekly (ticket) semanal

welcome benvindo, benvinda

west oeste

what que

wheelchair a cadeira de rodas; ~ **ramp** a rampa para cadeira de rodas

when quando

where onde

white branco, branca

who quem

wife a mulher [a esposa]

window a janela; **(store)** a montra

window seat o lugar à janela

windshield o pára-brisas

windsurfer a prancha à vela

wireless sem fios; ~ **internet** internet sem fios; ~ **internet service** serviçode internet sem fios; ~ **phone** telephone sem fios

with com

without sem

woman a mulher

wool a lã

work *v* **(job)** trabalhar; **(function)** funcionar

wrap *v* embrulhar

wrist o pulso

write *v* escrever

wrong errado, errada

Y

year o ano

yellow amarelo, amarela

yes sim
young jovem
youth hostel a pousada [o
albergue] da juventude

Z

zebra crossing [BE] a passadeira
[a faixa de pedestres]
zero zero
zone a zona
zoo o jardim zoológico, o zoo
Portuguese– English

A

à tarde p.m.
a abadia abbey
o abajur lampshade
aberto open
o abraço hug
abril April
acampar camp
o acesso para deficientes access for handicapped
achados e perdidos lost and found
o açougue butcher (Braz.)
o acrílico acrylic
o açúcar sugar
adiante ahead
a admissão admissions
o advogado attorney
o aeroporto airport
a agência de câmbio currency exchange office
a agência de viagens travel agent
agora now
agosto August
a água potável drinking water
o albergue de juventude youth hostel
a aldeia village
a alergia allergy
alérgico allergic

a alfândega customs
o algodão cotton
alguém someone
o alojamento accommodations
alpinismo mountaineering
aluga-se for rent
alugam-se carros car rental
aluguer [aluguel] de bicicletas bicycle rental
amanhã tomorrow
a ambulância ambulance
o andebol handball
antiguidades antiques
aquecer warm
a areia sand
o armazém department store
o ascensor elevator
o aspirador vacuum
a assinatura signature
atender answer
o atendimento admissions
o atendimento ao cliente customer service
atrasado delayed
o atrelado trailer
a auto-estrada highway [motorway]
o autocarro bus
automático automatic

o **automóvel** car
o **avião** plane
o **aviso** warning

B

a **bagagem** baggage [luggage]
o **balcão de registo** check-in counter
o **balcão de informações**
  information desk
a **balsa** ferry (Braz.)
o **banco** bank
o **banheiro** bathroom [toilets]
  (Braz.)
o **banho** bath
o **barbeiro** barber
o **barco** boat
o **barco salva-vidas** lifeboat
o **basebol** baseball
o **basquetebol** basketball
o **beijo** kiss
bemvindo welcome
a **biblioteca** library
a **bicicleta** bicycle
o **bilhete electrónico** e-ticket
o **bilhete semanal** weekly ticket
a **bilheteira** ticket office
o **bilhete** ticket
os **bolsos** pockets
a **bomba** pump
a **bomba de gasolina** gas [petrol]
  station

os **bombeiros** fire department
  [brigade]
as **botas de ski** ski boots
o **boxe** boxing
o **briberom** baby bottle

C

o **cabeleireiro** hairdresser
o **cabeleireiro de homens** barber
o **cabelo** hair
a **cachoeira** waterfall (Braz.)
a **cadeira de rodas** wheelchair
a **caixa** cashier
o **calçado** shoes
a**calculadora** calculator
o **calor** heat
as **calorias** calories
a **câmara** municipal town hall
o **câmbio** currency exchange
  office
o **camião** truck
o **caminho** path
a **camioneta** bus [coach]
o **camping** campsite
o **campo de desportos** playing
  field
a **cana de pesca** fishing rod
o **canal** canal
cancelado canceled
o **candeeiro** lamp
o **capacete** helmet

a **capela** chapel
o **cardápio** menu (Braz.)
o **carnaval** carnival
a **carne** meat
o **carro** car
a **carta regist[r]ada** registered letter
o **cartão** business card
a **carteira** wallet
a **casa** house
a **casa de banho** bathroom
a **casa de câmbio** currency
  exchange office
o **casaco** coat
o **castelo** castle
a **catedral** cathedral
o **cavalo** horse
a **caverna** cave
o **cemitério** cemetery
o **cêntimo** cent
o **centro comercial** shopping mall
  [shopping centre]
o **centro da cidade** downtown area
o **centro desportivo** sports center
o **centro do povo** town square
a **cerveja** beer
o **chá** tea
o **chalé** cottage
a **chamada gratuita** toll-free call
a **charcutaria** delicatessen
a **chave** key
as **chegadas** arrivals (airport)

a **chupeta** pacifier
o **churrasco** barbecue
a **chuva** rain
o **chuveiro** shower
a **cidade** city
a **cidade antiga** old town
o **cigarro** cigarette
o **cinema** movie theater [cinema]
a **cirurgia** surgery
a **clínica de saúde** health clinic
o **cobre** copper
o **código de área** area code
o **colete de salvação** life jacket
a **colina** hill
com with
com chumbo leaded
o **comboio rápido** express train
o **comboio suburbano** local train
o **combustível** fuel
completo full
o **comprimido** pill
o **computador** computer
a **comunhão** communion
o **condicionador** conditioner
a **confeitaria** pastry shop
congelado frozen
os **consertos** repairs
constipado constipated
a **conta corrente** checking
  [current] account
a **conta de poupança** savings

account
o **conteúdo** contents
o **controle de**
  passaportes passport control
o(s) **correio(s)** post office
o **correio azul** express mail
o **correio normal** regular mail
a **corrente** lock
os **cosméticos** cosmetics
a **costa** coast
o **couro** leather
o **credifone** phone card
a **criança** child
o **cuidado** caution
os **cuidados intensivos** intensive
  care

D

a **dança** dance
a **data** date
a **data de nascimento** date of
  birth
o **deck de automóveis** parking
  deck (Braz.)
de ida e volta round-trip [return]
o **dentista** dentist
a **depilação a cera** waxing
o **depósito** refund
o **depósito de bagagem** baggage
  check
descartável disposable

o **desconto** discount
desembarque arrivals (airport)
o **desentupidor** plunger
o **deserto** desert
despachar check (baggage)
o **desporto** sports
o **destino** destination
o **desvio** detour [diversion]
o **detergente** detergent
devagar slow
a **devolução** refund
Dezembro December
os **dias úteis** weekdays
os **dicionários** dictionaries
a **dieta** diet
o **dietético** health food
digital digital
o **dique** dam
a **direcção** address
dirija com cuidado drive carefully
dissolver dissolve
a **distância** distance
os **doces** candy [sweets]
os **documentos de regist[r]o**
  registration papers
doméstico domestic
o **domingo** Sunday
a **dor** pain
a **drogaria** drugstore
a **duna** dune

E

o elevador elevator
em construção under construction
em serviço occupied
a embaixada embassy
a embalagem perdida non-returnable
o embarque departures (airport)
a ementa menu
a ementa turística tourist menu
a emergência emergency
empurrar push
encerrado closed
a encosta perigosa dangerous slope
o endereço address
engraçado cute
a enseada bay
a entrada entrance
a entrada proibida no entry
entrar enter
a entrega de bagagem baggage claim
as entregas deliveries
o equipamento de mergulho diving equipment
os equipamentos eletrónicos electronic goods
o ervanário health food store
a escada rolante escalator
as escadas stairs
escalar climbing

a escarpa cliff
a escola school
o escritório de achados e perdidos lost-and-found office
a especialidade da casa house specialty
a especialidade da região local specialty
o espectáculo show
o espectador spectator
a esquadra da polícia police station
o esqui aquático waterskiing (Braz.)
a esquiagem skiing (Braz.)
os esquis skis (Braz.)
os esquis aquáticos water skis (Braz.)
esta noite this evening
a estação station
a estação de caminhos de ferro train station
a estação de metro subway station
a estação de serviço gas [petrol] station
a estação de ferroviária train station (Braz.)
a estação rodoviária bus [coach] station
o estacionamento parking lot [car park]

o **estacionamento para clientes** customer parking
estacione aqui park here
o **estádio** stadium
a **estância turística** tourist resort
o **estanho** can
a **estátua** statue
a **estrada** road
a **estrada em construção** road under construction
a **estrada fechada** road closed
o **estrangeiro** foreign
a **estreia** premiere
o **estreitamento de rua** narrow road
o **estuário** estuary
exclusivo para residentes residents only
exclusivo para pedestres pedestrians only
exclusivo para pessoal autorizado authorized vehicles only
a **excursão** tour
exige-se a identificação proof of identity required
a **exposição** exhibition
o **extintor (de incêndios)** fire extinguisher

F

a **fábrica** factory

a **fábrica manual** made by hand
fala-se inglês English spoken
a **farmácia** drugstore
o **farol** lighthouse
a **fazenda** farm (Braz.)
a **febre** fever
fechado closed
a **feira** fair
a **feira popular** amusement park
feito à mão handmade
o **feriado nacional** national holiday
o **ferroviário** railroad (Braz.)
Fevereiro February
o **fim** end
o **fim de auto-estrada** end of highway [motorway]
a **floresta** forest
o/a **florista** florist
o **fogo de artifício** fireworks
a **fonte** fountain
a **forma** form
a **fortaleza** fortress
o **forte** fort
a **fotocópia** photocopy
a **fotografia** photography
a **fralda** diaper [nappy]
a **frente** front
fresco fresh
a **fronteira** border crossing
a **fruta** fruit

fumar v smoke
os fumadores smoking (area)
os fumantes smoking (area) (Braz.)
o futebol soccer [football]
o futebol americano American
   football

G

a galeria de arte art gallery
a garagem garage
a garantia guarantee
a gare platforms
a gasolina gas [petrol]
genuíno genuine
o/a gerente manager
a gilete razor (Braz.)
o ginásio gym
o glúten gluten
o golfe golf
a gota drop
grande large
grátis free
gratuito free
a gravata tie
a grávida pregnant
a grelha de churrasco barbecue
o grelhado grilled
a gruta cave
guardar save
o guia de viagem travel guide

H

o helicóptero helicopter
o hipismo horseback riding
o hipódromo racetrack [racecourse]
hoje today
o hóquei hockey
o hóquei no gelo ice hockey
o horário schedule [timetable]
o horário comercial business hours
o horário de abertura opening
   hours
o horário de visitas visiting hours
o hospital hospital
o hotel hotel

I

ida e volta round-trip [return]
a igreja church
a ilha island
o IVA imposto de venda sales tax
   [VAT]
incluído included
incluído no preço included in the
   price
o indicativo code
o infantário kindergarten
as informações information
as informações turísticas tourist
   information
o ingrediente ingredient
o início de auto-estrada highway

[motorway] entrance
inocente innocent
inquebrável unbreakable
inserir v insert
insosso bland
as instruções instructions
integral whole wheat
interdito ao trânsito traffic-free zone
interessado interested
internacional international
introduzir introduce
o inverno winter
o IVA sales tax [VAT]

J

Janeiro January
a janela window
o jardim garden
o jardim botânico botanical garden
o jardim zoológico zoo
a joalharia jeweler
o jogo match
Julho July
Junho June

L

a lã wool
o lago lake
a lancha motorboat

os lanches snacks
o largo square
os lacticínios dairy products
a lavagem de carros car wash
a lavagem de roupa laundry facilities
a lavandaria laundromat [launderette]
la avandaria a seco dry-cleaner
lavar a seco dry-clean only
lavável à máquina machine washable
a lembrança souvenir
a lente lens
as lições lessons
a lima nail file
o limite da cidade city limits
o limite de bagagem baggage allowance
a limpeza cleaning
a língua language
a língua estrangeira foreign language
a linha platform
a linha aérea airline
a linha de bonde tram (Braz.)
a linha férrea railroad [railway]
a liquidação clearance sale
o líquido liquid
Lisboa Lisbon
a lista menu

a **lista telefónica** directory
a **lista de preços** price list
o **litoral** coast
a **livraria** bookstore
livre vacant
o **livrete** car registration papers
o **loção para depois da barba** after-shave lotion
a **loja de antiguidades** antique store
a **loja de artigos de desporto** sporting goods store
a **loja de brinquedos** toy store
a **loja de departamentos** department store
as **lojas duty-free** duty-free store
a **lotação esgotada** sold out
a **lotaria** lottery
a **louça** china
o **lugar à janela** window seat
o **lugar na asa** aisle seat
o **luxo** luxury

M

a **madeira** wood
as **madeixas** highlights
o **maestro** conductor
magro fat-free
Maio May
mais more
mais devagar slower

mais rápido faster
as **malas** luggage [baggage]
mandar send
os **mandriões** loafers
o **mapa da cidade** city map
o **mapa dos arredores** area map
a **máquina fotográfica** camera
o **mar** sea
Março March
as **massas** noodles
a **mata** wood
a **maternidade** maternity
a **matrícula do automóvel** license plate [registration] number
o **médico** doctor
médio medium
o **menu** menu
o **menu turístico** tourist menu
o **mercado** market
as **mercadorias** goods
as **mercadorias isentas** duty-free goods
a **mercearia** grocer
mergulhar diving
o **metro** subway [underground]
a **mina** mine
a **missa** mass
o **mobiliário** furniture
a **moeda** coin
o **moinho** mill
o **moinho de vento** windmill

molhada wet
o molusco shellfish
a montanha mountain
o montanhismo mountaineering
o monte hill
o monumento monument
o monumento comemorativo (war) memorial
o mosteiro monastery
a moto de montanha mountain bike
a motorizada motorcycle
os móveis furniture
as mudanças manual shift
a mudança de óleo oil change
mudar change
a mulher woman
a muralha da cidade city wall
o muro wall
o museu museum
a música music
a música ao vivo live music
a música clássica classical music
a música folk folk music
a música pop pop music

N

nacional national
nacionalidade nationality
nada a declarar nothing to declare
não entre keep out

não fumadores non-smokers
não fumantes non-smokers (Braz.)
não fumar no smoking
não funciona out of order
o Natal Christmas
navegação à vela sailing
o navio ship
a neve snow
o nome name
a nome de família last name
o nome de solteira maiden name
Novembro November
novo new
as nozes nuts
o número de telefone telephone number
o número do passaporte passport number

O

as obras construction
o oculista optician
ocupado occupied
a oferta especial special offer
a oficina office
o óleo oil
o ônibus bus (Braz.)
o ônibus elétrico tram (Braz.)
o operador operator
a ordem de pagamento money order

a orquestra orchestra
a ourivesaria goldsmith
o ouro gold
o outono fall [autumn]
Outubro October

P

o paço palace
a padaria bakery
o país country
o palácio palace
o palácio da justiça law court
o palco stage
o pão bread
o papel higiénico toilet paper
o papel reciclado recycled paper
a papelaria stationery store
para microondas microwaveable
para uso externo external use only
a paragem de autocarro bus stop
o parapente gliding
o pára-quedas parachuting
pare stop
a parede wall
o parque park
o parque de campismo campsite
o parque de diversões
  amusement park
o parque de estacionamento
  parking lot [car park]
o parque nacional national park

o parque para clientes customer
  parking
o parque privativo private parking
as partidas departures (airport)
as partidas internacionais
  international departures
a Páscoa Easter
a passadeira crosswalk
  [zebra crossing]
o passageiro passenger
as passagens (airplane) tickets
o passaporte passport
o passe mensal monthly ticket
o passeio walkway
o passeio panorâmico scenic route
o passeio a cavalo horseback
  riding
o passeio com guia guided tour
o passeio circular round trip
a pastelaria pastry shop
a pastilha lozenge
a patinagem no gelo ice skating
os patins skates
pedestre pedestrian (Braz.)
o pediatra pediatrician
a pedicure pedicure
o peito chest
a peixaria fish store [fishmonger]
a pensão bed & breakfast
os peões pedestrian
pequeno small

o **pequeno-almoço** breakfast
o **percurso da natureza** nature trail
o **percurso de bicicleta** bike trail
o **percurso panorâmico** scenic route
perdido lost
o **perigo** danger
perigoso dangerous
permanecer v stay
a **pérola** pearl
perto near
a **pesca** fishing
o **pico** peak
a **pílula** pill
o **PIN** PIN
pintado de fresco wet paint
a **piscina** swimming pool
a **pista de corrida** racetrack (Braz.)
a **pista de ônibus** bus lane (Braz.)
a **pista escorregadia** slippery road (Braz.)
a **pista fechada** road closed (Braz.)
a **pista simples** two-way traffic (Braz.)
o **planador** gliding
o **planetário** planetarium
o **pneu** tire [tyre]
o **poço** well
pode cozinhar cooking facilities
a **polícia** police

a **polícia de trânsito** traffic police
a **poltrona** seat
a **pomada** ointment
o **pomar** orchard
a **ponte** bridge
a **ponte baixa** low bridge
a **ponte estreita** narrow bridge
a **ponte levadiça** drawbridge
o **ponto de ônibus** bus stop (Braz.)
o **ponto de táxi** taxi stand [rank] (Braz.)
por favor please
a **porta** door
o **porta-moedas** purse
a **porta de embarque** boarding gate
a **porta de incêndio** fire door
a **portagem** toll
o **portão** gate
a **porta automática** automatic door
o **porto** port
o **posto de ambulância** ambulance station
o **posto de gasolna** gas [petrol] station (Braz.)
a **pousada** guest house
o **povoado** village
a **praça** square
a **praça de táxis** taxi stand
a **praia** beach

a praia de nudismo nudist beach
a prancha de surf[e] surfboard
a prata silver
o prato do dia dish of the day
o preço price
preferencial yield [give way]
a primavera spring
a primeira classe first class
Primeiro do Ano New Year's Day
  (Braz.)
o primeiro nome first name
os primeiros socorros first aid
a prioridade priority
privado private
os produtos de limpeza cleaning
  products
o produto dietético health food
proibida a entrada no entry
proibido forbidden
proibido acampar no camping
proibido estacionar no parking
proibido fumar no smoking
o pronto socorro-emergência
  accident and emergency
o propósito purpose
provar v taste
o próximo next
puxar pull

Q

a quantia fare

quarta-feira Wednesday
o quartel de bombeiros fire
  station
o quarto duplo double room
o quarto para alugar room to rent
quatro estrelas four star
a queda de água waterfall
a queda de pedras falling rocks
o quilómetro kilometer
a quinta farm
quinta-feira Thursday
o quiosque de jornais newsagent

R

os raios-x x-ray
a rampa ramp
a receita federal customs control
a recepção reception
o recibo receipt
reciclado recycled
reduza a velocidade slow down
o reembolso refund
as refeições meals
o regente conductor (music)
a região region
o relicário shrine
as reparações repairs (car)
a represa dam
o rés-do-chão first floor
reservado reserved
a reserva reservation

o **reservatório** reservoir
residencial guest house
o **restaurante** restaurant
retire fundos withdraw money
retire o bilhete take ticket
retornar v return
a **revista** magazine
a **ribeira** stream
o **rio** river
o **rochedo** cliff
o **rolo** film (camera)
a **rota alternada** alternate route
a **rotunda** traffic circle
  [roundabout]
a **roupa interior** underwear
a **rua** street
a **rua fechada ao trânsito** road
  closed
a **rua principal** main road
a **rua com sentido único** one-way
  street
as **ruínas** ruins

S

sábado Saturday
o **sabonete** soap
o **saco** bag
a **saída** exit
a **saída de emergência**
  emergency exit
o **sal** salt

a **sala de operações**
  operating room
s **sala de concertos** concert hall
s **sala de espera** waiting room
o **saldo** sale
a **salsicharia** delicatessen
o **salva-vidas** lifeguards
o **sapato** shoe
a **sé** cathedral
o **secador de cabelo** hair dryer
a **seda** silk
a **segunda classe** second class
o **segundo andar** second floor
segunda-feira Monday
os **segundos** seconds
a **segurança** security
o **seguro** insurance
o **selo** stamp
sem açúcar sugar-free
sem álcool alcohol-free
sem cafeína caffeine-free
sem chumbo unleaded
sem gordura fat-free
sem sal salt-free
o **semáforo** traffic light
a **semana** week
a **senha** ticket
as **senhoras** ladies
a **serra** mountain range
o **serviço** service charge
o **serviço a clientes** customer

service
o serviço de quarto room service
o serviço incluído service included
Setembro September
sexta-feira Friday
o silêncio silence
a sinaleira traffic light (Braz.)
só com dinheiro cash only
a sobremesa dessert
a soirée evening performance
o solário sun lounge
o solo escorregadio slippery road surface
o solteiro single (room)
o sombreiro umbrella (Braz.)
a sopa soup
sos emergency services (Port.)
o spa spa
o suco fruit juice (Braz.)
o supermercado supermarket

T

os talheres utensils [cutlery]
o talho butcher
a tarifa rate
a tarifa de pedágio toll (Braz.)
a tarifa mínima minimum charge
a taxa de serviço service charge
o táxi taxi
o taxímetro taxi meter
o teatro theater

o teatro ao ar livrea open-air theater
o teatro infantil children´s theater
o teleférico chair lift
o telefone telephone
o telefone de emergência emergency telephone
o telefone público public telephone
o telefone residencial home phone number
os temperos spices
a tenda tent
o ténis tennis
a terapia intensiva intensive care
terça-feira Tuesday
o terminal terminal
a tipografia printing
as toalhas linen
tóxico toxic
o tráfego lento slow traffic
o trajecto do autocarro bus route
o trampolim diving board
transferir transfer
o trânsito impedido closed to traffic
transportar carry
o tratamento treatment
o travão brake
o travão de emergência emergency brake

o trem expresso express train (Braz.)
o trem local local train (Braz.)
to revo intersection (Braz.)
o trigo wheat
o trolley-carro tram
o túnel tunnel
o turismo tourist information office

U

a universidade university
os utensílios de cozinha kitchen equipment
os utensílios domésticos household goods

V

o vagão-cama sleeping car
o vagão restaurante dining car
a vaga vacancy (Braz.)
vago vacant
o vale valley
o vale postal money order
válido valid
a varanda balcony
os vegetais vegetables
o veículo vehicle
o veículo lento slow vehicle
o veleiro sailboat
a velocidade máxima maximum speed limit

a venda de bilhetes ticket office
venenoso poisonous
o verão summer
o verdadeiro real
o verdureiro fruit and vegetable store (Braz.)
o vestuário fitting room
a via de dois sentidos two-way traffic
a via de sentido único one-way street
a via rápida highway [motorway]
a via turística scenic route
o vidro glass
o vidro reciclado recycled glass
a vila town
o vilarejo village
as vinhas vineyard
o vinho do porto port (wine)
o vinho wine
a visita guiada guided tour
o voleibol volleyball
o vôo flight

Z

a zona aduaneira customs zone
a zona comercial business district
a zona de pedestres pedestrian zone
a zona histórica historic area
a zona residencial residential zone